PAIN IS INEVITABLE
MISERY IS OPTIONAL

PAIN IS INEVITABLE MISERY IS OPTIONAL

HYRUM W. SMITH

WITH GERRELD L. PULSIPHER

DESERET
BOOK

SALT LAKE CITY, UTAH

Library of Congress Cataloging-in-Publication Data

Smith, Hyrum W.
    Pain is inevitable, misery is optional / Hyrum W. Smith with Gerreld L. Pulsipher.
       p.   cm.
    Includes index.
    ISBN 1-57345-450-8 (alk. paper)
    1. Suffering—Religious aspects—Church of Jesus Christ of Latter-day Saints.   2. Pain—Religious aspects—Church of Jesus Christ of Latter-day Saints.   3. Church of Jesus Christ of Latter-day Saints—Doctrines.
I. Pulsipher, Gerreld L.   II. Title.

BX8643.S93S65 2004
248.8'6—dc22   2003025380

Printed in the United States of America   18961-6429
R. R. Donnelley, Crawfordsville, IN

10 9   8   7   6   5   4   3   2   1

CONTENTS

ACKNOWLEDGMENTS

In addition to my good wife, Gail, and our children, there are four people I feel a need to acknowledge in helping me create this book:

Gerreld Pulsipher has been a close and dear friend for many years. Jerry saw me through many of the most painful events of my life in recent years, and he knows much about how I have felt during those experiences. He also played a major role in helping me write three books for the business world, *The Ten Natural Laws of Time and Life Management*, *What Matters Most*, and *The Modern Gladiator*. This book is considerably different from those in substance and tone. Without Jerry's input and skill, this book would not exist. His contribution to this work is so huge that I have insisted that his name be on the title page of the book with mine. Jerry is a man without guile, and the world needs more like him.

Annie Oswald is also a dear and trusted friend. Without her natural feel for what is appropriate and readable, I would be in real trouble. Her editing skills are unmatched. She has a marvelous record in helping a number of authors produce wonderful books. I am so grateful for her tireless efforts, encouragement, and support for this work throughout its preparation.

Sheri Dew must take responsibility for encouraging me to write this book. A great and longtime friend, Sheri kept after me to put all this in writing. There were times when I wondered if we could ever say anything of value to others in this book. But Sheri has been supportive and encouraging through it all, and I have learned much about myself in the process. Thank you, Sheri, for your support and faith in me.

Lastly, this book would not have been possible without the foundation given to me as a young missionary by Elder Marion D. Hanks, my mission president. President Hanks has had more impact on me for good than any other person I have known in my adult life. I learned at his feet in England more than forty years ago as a young missionary, when I first discovered in myself a serious desire to teach. I ached to be able to communicate as well as he did and to have his command of language and the scriptures. I was, and still am, in awe of his ability to lead students to their own minds and to the truths of the restored gospel as contained in the holy scriptures. Through the years President Hanks has stuck by me through many challenges, always there for me as a mentor and a trusted friend. There are no words to express my gratitude to him for his love and example.

One concluding thought: The gospel is true, the one sure guide and road map that will take us back to our heavenly home and our Heavenly Father. While the gospel is true and without error, I also know from experience that I am far from infallible. Therefore, the thoughts offered in this book are my own, and to the degree that they fall short of the perfection of our Heavenly Father and his Beloved Son, I accept full responsibility. I am receiving no royalties from the sale of this book. I simply hope my story can help others.

———◆◆◆———

ANGUISH AT 3:00 A.M.

In 2002, December 6 fell on a Friday. The evening before, I had gone to bed early, all too aware of the long day that lay ahead. By 1:00 A.M. I realized that sleep was not going to come, so I wandered alone through the darkened house. The tiny crescent moon had set, and the night seemed darker than usual outside. Pacing the floor in the wee hours of the morning is an activity I had come to know well in the past several years, but for the next three hours I paced the floor with a sense of anxiety that rose with every passing minute.

Four days earlier, I had received a telephone call from one of "my" missionaries. In the late 1970s, I had served as mission president in the California Ventura Mission, and I was stunned when this missionary informed me that Lowell Hansen, one of our elders, had taken his life the night before, leaving behind a wife and eight children. The rest of that day I thought of Elder Hansen and the experiences we had shared more than two decades ago in the mission field, and my emotions were very close to the surface. My heart went out to his wife and children, and I wondered how they were dealing with the pain of this tragedy.

The next day, Tuesday, I received another telephone call—

1

this time from Emma Jean, Elder Hansen's wife. She explained some of the circumstances surrounding his death and asked if I would be willing to be the main speaker for his funeral in the little Idaho farming community where they had lived for several years. I was honored that she would want me to do so, and I told her that I was most willing to accept the invitation.

Now, as I walked the halls of my home on a dark and sleepless night, I was feeling some pain of my own. My mind was racing. In little more than three hours, I was going to get on a plane with Gail, my wife; fly to Idaho Falls; rent a car; and then drive to the small town where the funeral would take place. Ever since Emma Jean's call, I had agonized over what I knew would be one of the most difficult, important, and challenging speaking assignments I had ever been given.

Endless questions coursed through my soul: Why would the family ask me to speak at this funeral? What could I possibly say that would ease the pain or be a source of help or comfort, especially given the tragic circumstances of Lowell's untimely death? Why had I in particular been asked to speak? What could I offer through the spoken word that would help this family, whose departed husband and father I had seen only occasionally, at best, in the years since the mission? Surely someone who knew Lowell and Emma Jean and their family better than I did would be a more appropriate speaker for this occasion. How could I help alleviate the pain that must be weighing down the hearts and minds of the family and friends who would attend the funeral? Why would Elder Hansen have taken his life? What was he thinking? What were his children thinking? What were they feeling? My mind kept running in circles. How could I, Hyrum Smith, say anything that would be meaningful?

This was an especially agonizing problem for me because public speaking is something I do for a living. I have spoken to audiences all over the world and given speeches in almost every major city in the United States. And here I was, finding myself literally without words, trying to figure out what to say that would help.

As I paced I realized that a major source of my anguish had to do with the fact that I myself had just completed a long and painful four-year journey to regain my membership in the Church and, later, to have my priesthood blessings reinstated. My mind vividly recalled much of the anguish and uncertainty I experienced as my soul was patiently tutored by the Holy Spirit. There was the defining moment, as I listened to a general conference address in October 1998, when I knew that I had been living a lie for several years, that I could no longer hide from the Lord, and that I could not go on living that way. At that time, it became clear that the only thing that really mattered was to make sure my relationship with my Savior was right. I knew the road would be difficult, and I remembered the fear that I might lose everything that was dear to me—my wife, my eternal family, and my chance to return to my Father in Heaven and his Beloved Son.

In those early morning hours, I found myself reflecting on the entire process, not only the pain and anguish I had experienced but also the pain and anguish I had inflicted on my family, my wife, my children, and 640 former missionaries who had looked to me for an example. I found myself remembering the day-by-day process of putting my relationship back together with my Heavenly Father and repairing my relationship with my wife and children, with my colleagues at work, and with my missionaries, trying to restore relationships and heal the wounds I had caused. I found myself remembering the anguish of that, the sorrow I had experienced, and the sometimes overwhelming feeling that I would never survive it all.

I remembered the pain and anguish of people who loved and respected me and expected better of me. I remembered the look in the eyes of my children as I explained to them what their father had done.

That early morning as I paced the floor, I remembered the lessons I had learned about forgiving and forgiveness, and how incredibly difficult it is for us mortals to forgive. I remembered too how difficult it was to forgive myself, and, as I distanced myself from the transgression, I could remember how foolish I had felt and how amazed I was at the stupidity of what I had done. I wondered where my brain could possibly have been, and I marveled at how I had deceived myself over such a long period of time.

But not all of the memories in those early morning hours were painful. I thought again of the time when the incessant tide of pain began to subside, when I finally felt that I was able to communicate again with my Father in Heaven, and at long last, the joy of the moment when I knew that the Lord had forgiven me. I will never forget that moment—the relief from the anguish and the peace that came with it.

Following this came the memories of the day when, after all the proper procedures and interviews and approvals had been completed, I reentered the waters of baptism and, with my son Joseph officiating, received the cleansing and peace that come with that holy ordinance. I had reentered the gate and was once again on the strait and narrow path.

All of this was coursing through my soul, and it was now

about three-thirty in the morning. I still hadn't focused on what to say at the funeral. But I had a magnificent experience of remembering, of having the Spirit walk me through the whole experience I had gone through in those previous four years. And now, with the help of the Spirit, it finally came to me why I had been asked to speak at that funeral. All those memories—both the wrenching and the joyful—had not just been a self-indulgent exercise. I suddenly realized that I was perhaps profoundly qualified to speak at the funeral of this young man who had taken his own life. Lowell Hansen, my missionary, had made a mistake—a huge mistake, a most serious mistake—in taking his life. He wouldn't be able to restore his life, but like me, in spite of my terrible mistakes, he would be allowed to repent. That thought seared through my soul like a bolt of lightning.

In my heart I knew that Lowell Hansen would be allowed to go through the process I had just completed; he would be allowed to experience the same remorse about his mistake; he would be given the opportunity to make recompense with his Father in Heaven; he would be allowed to make things right with his family. It would not be easy, but in the Lord's due time he could be totally forgiven of his transgression. His was not an irrevocable mistake, just a colossal mistake, perhaps the ultimate piece of bad judgment. He had made a decision that only God has the right to make, but I felt certain that a loving Father in Heaven would still allow the healing of repentance in such cases. By bringing to recollection my own suffering over my sins and mistakes, the Lord had let me know exactly the kind of pain Lowell was feeling. And I also knew the path Lowell would have to take and the joyous destination to which that path would lead him.

As dawn approached I desperately wanted to convey to Lowell's family and friends in that funeral all these things I knew to be true, now more than ever. Could I explain to Lowell's wife and children that their husband and father had made a mistake and that he felt awful about that mistake? Could I help them understand that whatever caused him to take his life wasn't important; that what was really important was what he was thinking about now, and that the holy process he was entering would eventually remove the pain he was experiencing?

I knew with great certainty that even though we would be holding a funeral service for him in a few hours, Lowell Hansen was and is very much alive. His spirit now resides in the spirit world, where he can continue to grow and learn and repent. He is going though the same anguish we all go through after having made a big mistake.

Will the Lord allow him to repent? Yes. The Prophet Joseph Smith taught, "There is never a time when the spirit is too old to approach God. All are within the reach of pardoning mercy, who have not committed the unpardonable sin." (*Teachings of the Prophet Joseph Smith* [Salt Lake City: Deseret Book, 1976], 191.) And Joseph further explained that the Lord "knows the situation of both the living and the dead, and has made ample provision for their redemption, and the laws of the kingdom of God, whether in this world, or in the world to come." (Ibid., 220.)

So the opportunity for repentance exists in the spirit world as it does in mortality, though it may be more difficult for us in that realm than it is here. Will the Lord forgive Lowell? Of course, once he has truly repented and done all he can to pay the price—the same requirements all of us have here on earth.

Will his blessings eventually be restored? I believe they will, although only his Heavenly Father is fully aware of the opportunities to bless lives, especially the lives of his family, that Lowell has missed because of his premature departure from mortality.

These thoughts hit me like a ton of bricks. The important thing was that through the Savior's atonement, Lowell would be all right in the end. The answers were all there. The gospel of Jesus Christ answers all of these questions. I believed that, now more than ever before.

Would the Lord somehow give me the ability to share that message with the Hansen family? Of course, and I knew that with a surety. It was now about four o'clock in the morning, and I found myself very excited. The anguish and concern were gone; my inabilities and frailties were no longer a concern. I found myself eager for the new day, impatient to get on the plane. I drove faster than I really should have on the highway to the little community. Eager to be at the pulpit, I felt that the opening song went on forever. When it came time for me to speak, I stood before an audience that extended well back into the cultural hall, and I shared with gratitude and love what the Spirit had taught me earlier that morning.

So this is a book about pain, its important role in the eternal plan, and how we can deal with or alleviate it. I write not so much about physical pain but about the emotional and spiritual pain that in its extreme manifestations can wrack our souls with the torments of hell. I'm not the first nor will I be the last person who has experienced the excruciating pain that comes from transgression and feeling alienated from our Heavenly Father and his Beloved Son, our Savior. But I hope that some of the insights I have gained in my own process of repentance and dealing with its attendant pain will be a source of encouragement and comfort to others who find themselves in similar circumstances. It is my hope that in reading this book, you too will come to understand some great truths that the gospel so plainly encompasses but that we often don't understand until we are called upon to endure the pain that comes to everyone as part of the mortal experience.

Many years ago my own mission president, Elder Marion D. Hanks, taught me a profound truth: *Pain is inevitable, misery is optional.* We cannot avoid pain in our lives, but we do have control over how we respond to that pain. And we also have the divine help of the Holy Spirit in dealing with the pain that inevitably comes.

These eternal truths came to have special meaning to me in my own experience with pain during the events I relived that night in early December. Through those experiences, although painful to recall, I have come to better understand the role that pain plays in the eternal plan, how we can not only endure pain but also learn and grow from confronting it and, with the Lord's merciful help, overcome it.

Some pain comes from the fact that we live in an imperfect world. Bad things can and do happen to all of us, and most often these are not of our choosing or doing. But the most excruciating pain is that we inflict upon ourselves through the kind of self-deception that results in transgression of the natural laws the Lord has given us, and whose consequences we bring upon ourselves. Pain truly is inevitable for all of us, whether imposed or self-inflicted.

But it's also true that misery is not the inevitable result of pain but an option that we can choose or reject. Understanding the role of pain in the eternal plan, and some of the ways we learn and grow from it, while not being diverted or destroyed by it, is the subject of this book.

The Atonement is real, and its redemption is freely given to all of us if we will but avail ourselves of the Savior's mercy. Sadly, it took my own experience with the most difficult kinds of spiritual and emotional pain for me to fully learn this greatest of all truths that the gospel of Jesus Christ can teach us. I hope and pray that this book will help you avoid the kinds of self-deception that produce much of our pain, and to endure those pains you must endure with the assurance that there is divine light and love and joy at the end of the journey.

UNDERSTANDING AND CONFRONTING PAIN

Is there not wisdom in [the Lord's] giving us trials that we might rise above them, responsibilities that we might achieve, work to harden our muscles, sorrows to try our souls? Are we not exposed to temptations to test our strength, sickness that we might learn patience, death that we might be immortalized and glorified? If all the sick for whom we pray were healed, if all the righteous were protected and the wicked destroyed, the whole program of the Father would be annulled and the basic principle of the gospel, free agency, would be ended.

—Spencer W. Kimball

On October 19, 2001, little more than a month after the tragic events of September 11, 2001, my colleague Stephen Covey and I responded to a request for help from Mayor Rudolph Giuliani of New York City. We offered to do a free one-day workshop for the families of those affected by the 9/11 disaster, and this was something we felt truly impressed and honored to do.

When we arrived, Mayor Giuliani had arranged for a private tour of Ground Zero for Stephen and me. This occurred just about five weeks after the event. Sixteen hundred police officers, men and women, surrounded Ground Zero. You couldn't get down there without a police escort. About 5:15 in the morning, we found ourselves standing on the street in front of the place where the Marriott Hotel used to be. Only we weren't really standing on the street. We were standing on sixteen feet of compacted debris. As we stood there looking at this horrific disaster, the policeman who had been assigned to be our guide began to tell us his story.

He said, "You know, I was here that day. I was standing on the street right about where we are. I heard this big bang, I looked up, and all this stuff came flying out of the World Trade Center. It looked like paper until it hit the ground. It was fifty-foot I-beams, killing everybody they hit. I watched dozens of people jump from those towers, four of them holding hands. I saw my friends and colleagues lose their lives going up to save people while the towers came down. I saw eight people on the ground who were hit and killed by falling people."

I could barely comprehend what I was hearing. I couldn't imagine the kind of pain this man was feeling, and I knew that I could never fully feel this man's pain. Then he looked at me and said, "Mr. Smith, how many computers do you think there were in the World Trade Center?" I said, "Probably a lot."

He said, "We haven't found one!"

"How come?" I said.

"It was a 3,000-degree fire. It's still burning."

As he spoke, a crane pulled a tremendous I-beam out of the rubble; the end of the I-beam was dripping molten steel. Then he said, "When the second plane hit and the towers started to come down, we all thought we were dead. We dove under a car, and somehow we survived." I shook my head. I simply could not fathom all that this policeman had witnessed.

When we returned to the hotel at about seven-thirty that morning, we had to shower. We were covered with sooty ash—both structural and human. At eight o'clock the meeting began. Two thousand people were jammed into a ballroom designed for fifteen hundred. People were sitting on the floor. We began with two firemen and two policemen carrying in the American flag. Then sixty young women from the Harlem Girl's Choir sang three patriotic songs. I was very grateful that Stephen Covey had to speak first, because by this time I was an emotional mess.

When it was my turn to speak, I approached the front of the room, and before I reached the podium, a fireman, in uniform, about halfway back, stood up and yelled, "Mr. Smith, are you gonna tell us how to get up every morning when we just don't give a damn anymore?" That's how it started. It turned out to be one of the toughest yet ultimately most rewarding speaking experiences I've ever had.

Then these words flashed through my mind, and I said them out loud to that audience and to that fireman. They are the same words that are the title of this book: "Pain is inevitable, misery is optional." And this fireman seemed a little stunned, but he sat down and listened as I tried to help ease the pain.

I don't remember much else I said that day. The physical force of the combined pain in that room was overwhelming, almost suffocating, and I fervently prayed that I might say something that would alleviate even a tiny bit of their pain and provide some comfort. The whole experience brought the issue of the inevitability of pain into very sharp focus for me.

The fact is, bad things do happen to good people. They

just do. Hijacked airplanes fly into buildings; tornadoes and hurricanes cut a swath of destruction along their path; dams break and flood villages; accidents happen; young people die prematurely. And some people take their own lives. But how we choose to deal with the pain is ultimately a measure of who we are and a measure of our testimony of the atonement of our Lord and Savior, Jesus Christ.

That's why we have been given the gospel of Jesus Christ—to help us confront and deal with pain. Every one of the most serene, magnificent, wonderful people I've ever known has gone through some major pain in life.

WHERE DOES PAIN COME FROM?

Physical pain, while sometimes excruciating, is not always the most devastating pain we must deal with. With physical pain, we can often see or understand why it occurred, and even when we can't see or understand why it came to us, it is something we can deal with because it is physical and tangible. It generally hurts, perhaps even intensely, for a relatively short time. Then, as the body's nervous system shuts down the affected nerves or the effects of medication begin to take hold, the pain may lessen or eventually end.

Mental and spiritual pain are more problematic. We can't always identify what produces such pain, and it may be such that it never seems to end. It can hang over us like a dark cloud, causing depression and frustration, affecting everything we do. If unrelieved, it can warp our thinking, lead us into physical and mental illness, and, at the ultimate extreme, find us contemplating suicide. A special kind of mental and spiritual pain comes when we transgress the laws of God, as we sense the gap that we have created between ourselves and our

Heavenly Father. Such pain can be especially intense, and believe me, it's not the kind that can be relieved by aspirin.

Both of these kinds of pain come from two sources: pain the world inflicts upon us as an inherent part of our mortal experience, and pain we inflict upon ourselves, often by making mistakes or misjudgments about physical things or about moral and spiritual matters.

Whether imposed by the world or brought on by our own mistakes and misperceptions, much of our pain appears to be a by-product of a fundamental natural law at work in this mortal world. I'm talking about the law of entropy, a principle first identified by Isaac Newton that is the foundation of much of our scientific knowledge about why the world is as it is. In short, this natural law states: *Matter, after being energized by some outside force, tends to move from a state of high energy toward a state of low or no energy.*

Examples of this can be seen in the physical world all around us: hot soup gets cold, a fired bullet gradually loses velocity and drops to the ground, the warmth of the sun goes away at nightfall and the air cools, a loud sound fades away, a fire dwindles and dies, walls eventually crumble, new homes become run down, our fancy new automobile gets worn out and breaks down, and so on. This principle also applies to the living world. The life cycle of every living thing, whether measured in seconds or centuries, is an initial burst of life-giving energy followed by aging and eventual death.

Our own mortal lives, viewed in the gospel context, show this same law at work. The life energy released at conception produces a baby that rapidly grows to become a mature adult, followed by a long period of gradual physical decline that, even for the most fit and healthy, will eventually terminate in death. Life itself contains a built-in renewal factor that helps us continue to live for a time, but in the end we cannot escape the effects of the law of entropy, no matter how many vitamins or "stay young" potions we consume.

The law is also seen in human relationships and activities. A friendship that was fueled by mutual interests and trust may continue for a while, but if left untended, it will eventually become dormant or die. Communities that were founded around a single economic activity such as mining will feel the effects of entropy once the gold or silver runs out, accounting for the ghost towns we see around many parts of the western United States. Even nations and empires, born in much human energy and activity, will decay over time, losing their vitality and importance unless something or someone comes along to provide some form of renewal.

In fact, some form of intervention and renewal is the only reason the earth has not spun into a total state of entropy. Otherwise, Earth would be a dead planet, devoid of the energy and life that created and sustained the initial stages of its existence. To me, renewal is the great miracle of this planet and the means through which change and improvement are possible in a world where the natural tendency is toward decay and oblivion. Life itself, in its many forms, is the greatest earthly evidence of that miracle, which holds the promise for how we can most successfully deal with entropy and its resultant pain.

THE LAW OF RENEWAL

No doubt Satan believes that entropy is on his side, that the natural processes of death and decay set in motion in the garden of Eden will help him thwart the Father's plan. But in his wisdom, our Father in Heaven provided the means for entropy to be reversed through the law of renewal.

Like the law of entropy, the law of renewal can be seen in both living and nonliving things. It's an ongoing and little-appreciated miracle that the earth's supply of water is perpetually renewed through the water cycle. Ocean and air currents constantly renew the dynamism and energy of the earth's climatic patterns. In both plants and animals, entropy eventually results in death, but new seeds renew and sustain life on the planet.

The Lord himself has said, "Behold, I make all things new" (Revelation 21:5), and he has also stated, "This is my work and my glory—to bring to pass the immortality and eternal life of man" (Moses 1:39), which is itself a work of eternal renewal. And the ultimate example of the law of renewal at work is resurrection, whereby our Savior has made possible a rebirth into immortality for all who fall prey to the law of entropy and death. Even more profound evidence of the law of renewal in our personal lives is the process of redemption through the atonement of Jesus Christ, the cleansing, rebirth, and renewal of our souls so we can partake of eternal life.

In this context, we can see that a great deal of pain and despair in mortality is a by-product of the law of entropy at work, while hope and peace and joy are by-products of its opposite, the law of renewal.

Some of our pain is out of our control: We slip and fall on the ice, we just happen to be standing under something that collapses on us, we break a leg skiing, our automobile is broadsided by another car, one of our children is struck by a car and injured, or a loved one dies unexpectedly. Our very existence in mortality causes us pain.

In addition, we often bring pain upon ourselves. This can be as simple as missing the nail with a hammer and smashing a finger, or any of the other stupid or accidental things we do that cause injury or pain. We generally accept these moments as part of mortal life, and the pain they produce is usually short-lived.

But occasionally one of our mistakes produces more serious and lasting results, injuring another person or producing unintended consequences that last a lifetime. In these "if only I hadn't done that" instances, the pain can be excruciating and long lasting, providing the adversary with many opportunities to foster self-loathing and other destructive responses.

As I've learned by sad experience, we often bring pain upon ourselves in a way that is more sinister and less easy to detect: *self-deception.* I believe that deceiving ourselves is the cause of most transgression, especially among believing Latter-day Saints, who would not dream of breaking a major commandment of the Lord unless they had gone through some process of rationalization to justify what they were doing. Of all the causes of pain, this is perhaps the hardest to root out, simply because in self-deception we twist truth and distort reality to make immoral or unethical objectives seem acceptable or justified.

How Can We Best Deal With the Pains and Trials We Encounter?

Remember, just as the law of entropy is continually at work in the world, so also is the Lord's law of renewal, working by way of divine intervention in our behalf. Without that hope of renewal and all of the evidences of its reality that life provides, the mortal experience would be impossible to survive. If the law of entropy were the only governing law, there would be no hope of renewal and redemption.

Sometimes all we can do with world-inflicted pain is experience it, endure it, and learn what we can from it. Although we can take precautions, we cannot always avoid this kind of pain. The best we can expect is to adapt to it, grow because of it, and hold fast to the hope of eventual redemption through the saving power of the Atonement and the Lord's promise that someday all our pain will be taken away.

Although we may not realize it, self-inflicted pain does not have the same mortal-existence inevitability about it. With most pain that comes from simple mistakes and accidents, we can take extra care, be aware of dangers, and use other forms of caution and awareness to avoid or mitigate mistake-caused pain. For pain resulting from self-inflicted tragic mistakes that involve long-term consequences for another person, we can provide what restitution we are able to make, but we have to live with the consequences of our actions.

There is one kind of self-inflicted pain that we *can* do something about. This is the pain that comes from self-deception. I learned about this the hard way from my own transgressions, as described in the prologue. We'll talk more about avoiding pain through self-deception in chapter 6, but suffice it to say that there are ways to ensure that what you believe to be true about a situation is in fact in line with the reality of the situation. Wishing that things were different or feeling that they should be different than they really are can lead us into all kinds of trouble. Much transgression and the pain that results from it comes from erroneous beliefs like "I am a special case," "I am a product of poor upbringing," or "The Lord will overlook this one." This kind of thinking will only get us into deep water. When that happens, we find it easy to go our own way, either to our destruction or to the eventual realization that we have deceived ourselves and are far from the shore.

Sadly, we are not often taught or warned about the insidious subtlety of misperception and the way Satan can use it to deceive us. In the words of Nephi, "The devil cheateth their souls, and leadeth them away carefully down to hell." (2 Nephi 28:21.) I think this is part of what Nephi means when he says elsewhere that "they hearken not unto the counsel of God, for they set it aside, supposing they know of themselves, wherefore, their wisdom is foolishness and it profiteth them not. And they shall perish." (2 Nephi 9:28–29.)

THE STOCKDALE PARADOX

Let me conclude this chapter with an experience of a respected military man who has had a major impact on my own approach to pain. His experience and what he learned from it provide important insights that can help us better deal with difficult circumstances and accompanying mental and spiritual pain.

James Stockdale was an admiral and the highest-ranking military officer to be incarcerated in the infamous "Hanoi Hilton" as a prisoner of war during the Vietnam conflict. Admiral Stockdale, like all who underwent that ordeal, experienced a nightmare of physical as well as psychological and mental pain.

From this experience, he arrived at the same conclusion as Viktor Frankl, who was imprisoned at Auschwitz during the Second World War. In his book *Man's Search for Meaning,* Frankl describes how he came to the realization that although his captors could take everything material and physical away from him (including the lives of his family), they could not take away his thoughts or his choices as to how he would respond to his circumstances.

In Admiral Stockdale's case, he defined three basic types of people incarcerated with him in the prison, and what he observed about their attitudes and choices has since become known in military circles as the Stockdale Paradox. The three types of people were the pessimists, the optimists, and the realists. The pessimists saw the brutal facts of their situation and quit—they gave up. The optimists had boundless faith but ignored the brutal facts. And the realists saw and recognized the brutal facts but had faith they could be dealt with.

As I read Admiral Stockdale's account of his prison-camp experience, the thing that interests me most about these three groups is that almost all of the first two groups died in the camps at Vietnam—they never made it home.

I could understand why the pessimists didn't make it. They experienced the pain of the whole thing, saw the circumstances they had to face, and chose misery. They gave up the ghost—figuratively and literally.

But the second group stunned me. Why did the optimists die? I had always been taught that PMA—positive mental attitude—can get you through anything. The optimists died because they had all this faith and positive outlook but were not willing to look at the brutal facts of their situation. I can see them saying to each other things like "You know we'll be out of here by Christmas" or "We'll be rescued by Valentine's Day." Every rustle in the brush was the Marines coming to save them. And when every rustle in the brush wasn't the Marines coming to save them, and when they weren't out by

Christmas, and when they weren't rescued by Valentine's Day, they died. Over time, their spirits could not endure the constant rejection. They too ended up choosing misery and gave up.

But the realists survived. They saw the brutal facts. They knew that pain was inevitable. They said things like "We're in the middle of Southeast Asia. We're not going to be rescued for a long time. But you know what, guys? We'll stick together. We can handle this." They knew they had choices and options about how to deal with the pain they must endure. And not only did they deal with the pain, but many of them lived to return home.

So how do you view life's experiences? Do you, like the pessimists, see the brutal facts and give up? Do you see that since pain is inevitable, life is desolate, barren, and without meaning?

Or do you approach pain like the optimists—ignoring the facts, putting on a happy face, and pretending the bad stuff didn't happen? As an optimist, you can sometimes be in Never-Never Land—believing that pain happens only to the other guy or only if you aren't living right. Then you can be blindsided and devastated because you thought it could never happen to you.

I hope you can see the value in trying to be a realist—seeing the brutal facts and the pain but having faith that they can be dealt with. The realist can see the positive side of pain—misery is optional and is not, like pain itself, inevitable. An option other than misery is dealing with pain through faith, the help of the Holy Spirit, and hope in ultimate joy and redemption.

And that's what the rest of this book will deal with. We'll

look at the "merciful plan of the great Creator" (2 Nephi 9:6) and put pain in its eternal perspective. We'll talk about why pain is part of the plan, how to endure the pain that must be endured, how to grow and mature through pain, and how we can avoid self-deception and thus its resultant pain. We'll look at the role of the Holy Spirit in relieving pain, and we'll take a deeper look at the pain our Savior endured for us in bringing about the Atonement.

CHAPTER 2

"The Merciful Plan of the Great Creator"

If we looked at mortality as the whole of existence, then pain, sorrow, failure and short life would be a calamity. But if we look upon life as an eternal thing stretching far in the pre-mortal past and on into the eternal post-death future, then all happenings may be put in proper perspective. . . .

I am positive in my mind that the Lord has planned our destiny. Sometime we'll understand fully, and when we see back from the vantage point of the future, we shall be so satisfied with many of the happenings of this life that are so difficult for us to comprehend.

—Spencer W. Kimball

O n the day of my rebaptism, I was in the stake center with my family. We were all there. I was dressed in white, and my son Joseph was dressed in white sitting next to me. We were waiting for the service to begin. I was also sitting next to my three-year-old grandson, Sawyer. As I sat there waiting for the program to begin, Sawyer looked up at me and in a beautiful way said, "Grampy, why do you have to be baptized?"

That question from my young grandson took me in an instant back over all that had happened in those preceding months and years. I had an answer for Sawyer, but before I tell you what I said to him, let me first tell you about my ponderings during those many months that led to the much briefer answer I gave him.

For as long as I can remember, I have had to simplify things so I could better understand whatever it is I'm trying to learn. That's why the parables Jesus taught have always been so appealing to me. Through powerful mental imagery and conceptual links to universal aspects of everyday living, they make the profound truths he was teaching interesting and memorable.

Over the years I have used a simple metaphor to teach in a simple way what we know about where we came from, what happened to us in coming to mortality, and what Nephi of old called the "merciful plan of the great Creator" (2 Nephi 9:6), which makes it possible for us to return to God and, with our families, live with him forever.

My metaphor in understanding the plan is a bucket. Now, I realize that a bucket doesn't sound very profound; it doesn't exactly conjure up lofty images of divinely appointed plans being formulated in the heavenly councils. But it does provide a simple and illustrative way of understanding the overall framework of our eternal lives and some of the most important truths we need to understand for the mortal part of our journey. An understanding of our Father's plan is essential to understanding the pain and anguish we so often experience during the mortal portion of this divinely appointed plan.

When Adam and Eve found themselves in the Garden of Eden with God, they were not able to remember their pre-earth life, just as you and I are not able to remember our pre-earth life. But in the Garden of Eden, they were in the presence of God, perhaps even daily. Pain and sorrow, disease and decay were not yet part of their lives. They were not mortal at this point but were on the verge of so being. They were in the garden, with everything provided to meet their needs, and they enjoyed the direct guidance of their Father in Heaven.

When they made the choice—and it was a conscious choice—to partake of the forbidden fruit of the tree of knowledge of good and evil, they were not being willfully disobedient. They were facing an extremely difficult choice. On the one hand, they could have stayed in a state of perpetual innocence, enjoying the freely provided resources of the garden. But the scriptures and modern revelation tell us that Eve was the first to sense that remaining in their present state would not permit them to fulfill the other things their Heavenly Father had commanded them to do. Satan, in tempting her with the forbidden fruit, actually spoke the truth when he said, "God doth know that in the day ye eat thereof, then your eyes shall be opened, and ye shall be as gods, knowing good and evil." (Moses 4:11.)

Eve's response indicates that she glimpsed that knowing good from evil was important for them: "When the woman saw that the tree was good for food, and . . . to be desired to make her wise, she took of the fruit thereof, and did eat, and also gave unto her husband with her, and he did eat." (Moses 4:12.) "Many days" after they had been cast out of the garden, an angel sent by the Father and the bestowal of the Holy Ghost upon Adam verified that the choice, while painful, was necessary and right: "And in that day Adam blessed God and was filled, and began to prophesy concerning all the families of the earth, saying: Blessed be the name of God, for because of my transgression my eyes are opened, and in this life I shall have joy, and again in the flesh I shall see God. And Eve, his wife, heard all these things and was glad, saying: Were it not for our transgression we never should have had seed, and never should have known good and evil, and the joy of our redemption, and the eternal life which God giveth unto all the obedient." (Moses 5:10–11.)

As recounted in the scriptures, Adam and Eve were removed from their previous existence, their daily communion with and instruction from the Father and the Son, and they fell into mortality. This was a necessary change in their status, one that introduced not only death but also the contrasting emotions of joy and sorrow, pleasure and pain, happiness and misery, as well as the opposing states of health and sickness, holiness and wickedness, obedience and disobedience, and all the other manifestations Father Lehi attributed to the profound truth that "it must needs be, that there is an opposition in all things." (2 Nephi 2:11.)

This is where the bucket metaphor comes in. Adam and Eve's transgression is referred to in the scriptures and known in popular conception as the Fall. If we take that term figuratively, we can imagine that in leaving their existence with the Father, Adam and Eve fell to the bottom of a large, deep bucket we will call mortality. They were now mortals on earth, separated from God in a literal and physical way. Their quest then became that of getting back into the presence of God.

To help them do that, the Lord gave Adam and Eve (and, by extension, us) a plan to help them climb out of the bucket. In the forty-second chapter of Alma, this plan is referred to by four of its names: a plan of salvation, a plan of mercy, a plan of redemption, and a plan of happiness.

Why these names are used interchangeably becomes evident as we discover the basic elements of the plan. This plan, revealed to Adam and Eve after they left the garden, meant a great deal to them. It may have seemed even more important to them than to us, because though they could not remember their existence with God before coming to earth, they could remember the Garden of Eden. They could remember what it was like to be with God and Christ. And so when they were given a plan on how they could get back into that presence, I'm sure it was a serious, important thing, and, as stated in Moses 5:12, they taught it to their family: "Adam and Eve blessed the name of God, and they made all things known unto their sons and their daughters." Down through history, God's prophets have taught this plan, as did his Beloved Son during his ministry on the earth.

The plan has five simple but important elements to it. You could almost consider the plan as a ladder reaching into the bucket, with five rungs representing the five stages of the plan. The first three stages of the plan are possible for us to achieve in mortality. The last two are accomplished after death. This diagram of the bucket shows the relationships between the different steps on the ladder.

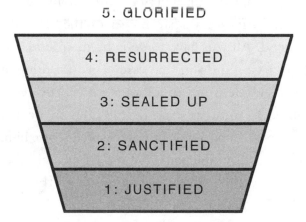

5. GLORIFIED

4: RESURRECTED

3: SEALED UP

2: SANCTIFIED

1: JUSTIFIED

Those are the five simple stages in this wonderful plan with the many names. Now let's talk about each element in greater detail.

1. ACHIEVE JUSTIFICATION

What does it mean to be justified? We read in many places throughout the scriptures that before anyone can enter into the presence of God, the demands of justice must be met. Our Heavenly Father demands justice, for he cannot look upon sin with the least degree of allowance. (Alma 45:16; D&C 1:31; see also Alma 42.) In simple words, if an eternal law is violated, there is an effect; the violation has to be paid for.

For example, if I borrow $10,000 from you and promise to pay it back in one year, at the end of the year you might reasonably come to me and say, "I'd like to have my $10,000." Suppose at that point I am unable to pay the $10,000 and so inform you. Now, is it fair that you don't get your money back? No, obviously. For justice to be met, you you must be paid in full. But if I'm incapable of paying you the $10,000, how is justice going to be met?

So let's suppose a third person comes along and says, "I'll tell you what, Hyrum. I'll pay this person the $10,000 if you'll be my friend. All you have to do is be my friend." What do you think I would do in that case? I would jump at it in a heartbeat. The demands of justice are met. You receive your $10,000 back, and that's fair. In this case, my debt was paid by someone else, and I would most assuredly owe him. In this particular situation, the person who paid my debt was for me a savior in a very real way, saving me from the immutable demands of justice.

There are three ways for justice to be met in matters relating to our eternal lives:

1. We can come down to this planet and commit no sin. If we do that, then justice has been met and nothing has to be paid for. At the end of the mortal journey we're pure, and we can go straight back into the presence of God. Judging from what I see of our collective and individual performance in mortality, I think we can safely write that one off for everyone except Jesus.

2. We can commit the sins that normal men and women commit and then pay for those sins ourselves. I think we can safely write that one off as well. The fact is, we're not capable of paying the price for most of the sins we commit.

3. We commit the sins and make mistakes that are inherent in being mortal, and we allow Jesus Christ, through the Atonement, to pay for those sins. That's really the only way. And Christ, as the only person who ever lived and himself committed no sin, is the only person who could accomplish such a universal atonement for all of us imperfect mortals who come to earth as part of the plan.

The first principles and ordinances of the gospel Joseph Smith so eloquently and clearly summarized in the fourth Article of Faith all fit neatly into the justification phase of this plan.

Faith comes first. Faith in what? Faith in Jesus Christ, that he can pay for our sins and provide the way for us to overcome our mortal imperfections.

Second, repentance. We forsake the sin, feel the godly sorrow for sin, seek our Father in Heaven's forgiveness, and refrain from repeating the sin.

Third, baptism. We go into the waters of baptism, formally

accepting Jesus' atonement, and making a commitment to take upon ourselves his name and live his commandments.

Fourth, to aid us in our quest, we are given the gift of the Holy Ghost, the Comforter, who will lead us to all truth and bring eternal truths back to our remembrance.

All of that happens in the justification stage of this plan. The result of this first and important phase of the gospel plan is that we obtain a remission of our sins.

2. BECOME SANCTIFIED

If, on our baptismal date, we happened to have slipped on the top step of the font, bumped our head, and died, we would have been in pretty good shape in terms of our eternal salvation, because at that point we were clean from the sins of the world. All of our sins had been forgiven, the demands of justice had been met, and we would have been ready for the higher phases of the plan. But fortunately or unfortunately, depending on your viewpoint, we survived our baptism day— we lived through it. That now makes necessary the second element of this wonderful plan, another ascending step in which we become sanctified. It is this stage that all of us are involved in presently if we are members of the Church and striving to retain the remission of sins that we obtained at baptism. The sanctification process, then, involves retaining that which we acquired the day we were baptized and thereafter working to become perfect in spirit and behavior.

I believe that about 90 percent of the scriptures we read in any of the four standard works deal with the sanctification process. Why? Because that's what we spend most of our lives trying to achieve, and the scriptures represent our Father's way of providing guidance and help to us on how we can become sanctified.

What does it mean to be sanctified? The *Webster's New World Dictionary* defines sanctification as "the state of being set apart as holy; consecrated; made free from sin." There are lots of other words that describe sanctification as being clean, purified, right before the Lord. It involves living the commandments. It's the continuation of the repentance process as we make further mistakes and avail ourselves of the Atonement to come back from those mistakes.

3. BE SEALED UP UNTO THE LORD

The Prophet Joseph Smith taught that it is actually possible to achieve sanctification in mortal life. If we did, we would find ourselves on the third step of our ladder out of the bucket, the step of being sealed up. I'm not talking about temple sealings, where we are sealed to our family and spouse for time and all eternity. True, the sealing of families is part of the sanctification process, but the sealing I'm talking about here is a different sealing, when the Lord seals us up unto eternal life—either in this life or the next. As Joseph Smith said, "After a person has faith in Christ, repents of his sins, and is baptized . . . and receives the Holy Ghost . . . , which is the first Comforter, then let him continue to humble himself before God, hungering and thirsting after righteousness, and living by every word of God, and the Lord will soon say to him, Son, thou shalt be exalted. When the Lord has thoroughly proved him, and finds that the man is determined to serve Him at all hazards, then the man will find his calling and his election made sure." (*Teachings of the Prophet Joseph Smith* [Salt Lake City: Deseret Book, 1976], 150.)

4. BE RESURRECTED

The fourth step of this plan is resurrection. At some point all of us will experience a mortal death, after which we'll go to the spirit world to await our resurrection. The resurrection—the reuniting of our spirit with an immortal body—will happen to everyone. This free gift is given by the Savior to every person who has ever lived; all will be resurrected, good or bad.

We are taught that there will be at least two resurrections. The first resurrection will be for those who have been successful in becoming sanctified and are ready and worthy to take the final step in the process, which is to become glorified, or, in other words, to be given eternal life. Abinadi, before being burned at the stake, declared, "The prophets, and all those that have believed in their words, or all those that have kept the commandments of God, shall come forth in the first resurrection; therefore, they are the first resurrection." (Mosiah 15:22.) Abinadi also included little children in this group.

The second resurrection is for less valiant souls who perhaps lost their way or didn't do particularly well at becoming sanctified. The quest, obviously, for each of us is to learn how to become sanctified through the help of our Father in Heaven so that we will come forth in that first resurrection.

5. BECOME GLORIFIED

The fifth and final step of this wonderful plan—the plan of salvation, mercy, redemption, and happiness—is to become glorified. I don't think any of us have even the tiniest glimpse of what this may be, but glorification is where we are assigned our place in the royal family of God, our Father in Heaven, who is the King. Most of us hope for the highest degree of the celestial kingdom, where we can reside with and walk and talk with God and be part of the ongoing process of creation and renewal forever.

If we have done our best at each stage of this eternal process, I believe that we will not stand alone when we present ourselves before God to be judged preparatory to being glorified. Father Lehi taught his children, "[Jesus Christ] is the firstfruits unto God, inasmuch as he shall make intercession for all the children of men; and they that believe in him shall be saved. . . . Wherefore, they stand in the presence of him, to be judged of him according to the truth and holiness which is in him." (2 Nephi 2:9–10.) Nephi assures us that "the keeper of the gate is the Holy One of Israel; and he employeth no servant there." (2 Nephi 9:41.)

Although the scriptures make no specific mention about the Savior pleading for us individually at the final judgment, my heart harbors the hope that when that moment comes, those who have been faithful will have as their advocate the Son of God, Jesus Christ.

If that is the case, I can imagine a conversation something like this, paraphrasing the words of the Savior in D&C 45:4–5: "Father, behold the sufferings and death of him who did no sin, in whom thou wast well pleased; behold the blood of thy Son which was shed. . . . Wherefore, Father, spare this my brother [or sister] who believes on my name, that he [or she] may come unto me and have everlasting life."

And I can imagine the Father saying, "If this is true, my Beloved Son, this person will be welcomed into my kingdom. Let them enter into the joy of their rest."

The thought of having to stand before God without the Savior as my advocate is what ultimately prompted me to do what I had to do to get back on the straight and narrow path, holding fast to the rod of iron. The rod of iron extends from the bottom of the bucket, through justification, and all the way up through glorification. It's the sure handrail that will guide us up and all the way out of the bucket, back to the glory of the eternal realms.

The bucket analogy is simple; it's not sophisticated or complicated, but it shows us the pathway from mortality to eternal life. It begins with our birth into mortality and then proceeds through achieving justification, becoming sanctified, being sealed up, being resurrected, and ultimately receiving glorification and eternal life with our Father in Heaven and our Savior. It is the plan that brought Adam and Eve back into the presence of their Father so they could again experience the daily contact with God that they had enjoyed at the beginning of their mortal experience.

As I have contemplated this marvelous plan, I'm regularly reminded that for a time I had to go in reverse—from the sanctification process back to the justification level before I could start the climb again. Having had to do that, and now having a clear memory of how difficult it was, my simple understanding of this profound plan has come to mean a great deal to me, more than ever before in my life. From my youth I've known the plan and thought I understood it. I've always believed in it. But now, having gone painfully through an important part of it again at my age, I am so grateful that the Lord has provided his children with this saving process. Knowing and understanding the plan has helped me better understand and endure the pain that has come when I've stumbled or had to retrace some of my steps.

That day as I waited to enter the baptismal font, I

responded to my little grandson's question about why I needed to be baptized. I said to Sawyer, "Sawyer, your grandfather made some mistakes. And because of those mistakes, I had to lose my membership in the Church. But Father in Heaven has allowed me to make those things right so I can be baptized again, have those sins forgiven, and come back into the Church and start again on the road back to Heavenly Father." It took me about fifteen seconds to teach him the basic premise underlying the plan. Sawyer looked at me, smiled, and said, "Oh," and the conversation was over.

I found myself getting very emotional at that point, realizing I had just taught the fundamentals of this simple plan to my grandson in fifteen seconds. It really is that simple. But even more important, it's all true. As I went into the waters of baptism that day, as my son Joseph baptized me, as I realized what was happening, I sensed the profound meaning of the plan much more clearly than I had when I was eight years old. It was one of the sweetest and most beautiful experiences of my life.

Just a little over a year after that, when a prophet of God laid his hands on my head and restored all of my priesthood blessings, this plan again came into my mind as I listened to the blessing that was pronounced. At that moment I knew for a certainty that many things are true and vitally important for us to understand. Achieving justification is important. It has to happen. Sanctification is a life's quest. Being sealed up, receiving the promise of eternal life, is an attainable goal, when we can know for a certainty that we will go back and be with our Father in Heaven. Resurrection is going to happen; it will come to us, like it or not.

Finally, we'll stand before our Father in Heaven, hopefully

with our Elder Brother, Friend, and Savior as our advocate, pleading our case before our Father: "Hyrum Smith's sins have been paid for. I have paid for them before the bar of justice. He has learned much in his journey since that time and has achieved sanctification. He has come forth through the power of the resurrection. Will you allow him into your kingdom?" And then, imagine our joy as God, our Eternal Father, welcomes us home.

There isn't anything more exciting than that to me. And that's what I live for at this point. I hope that's what we all live for. Teach your children the simplicity of the plan. It is not complicated. It is wonderfully simple, and it has been with us since the creation of the earth.

CHAPTER 3

WHY IS PAIN PART OF THE PLAN?

No pain that we suffer, no trial that we experience is wasted. It ministers to our education, to the development of such qualities as patience, faith, fortitude, and humility. All that we suffer and all that we endure, especially when we endure it patiently, builds up our char- acters, purifies our hearts, expands our souls, and makes us more tender and charitable, more worthy to be called the children of God.
— Orson F. Whitney

I do not believe that sheer suffering teaches. If suffering alone taught, all the world would be wise, since everyone suffers. To suffering must be added mourning, understanding, patience, love, openness, and the willingness to remain vulnerable.
— Anne Morrow Lindbergh

Before the world was created, the great council in heaven was convened to outline the plans for creating an earth, that the spirit children of our Father in Heaven might have the opportunity to go there, enter mortality, and go through the learning process necessary for them to become full members in the royal family of God. I love the description of those events as revealed in vision to Abraham: "There stood one among them that was like unto God, and he said unto those

39

who were with him: We will go down, for there is space there, and we will take of these materials, and we will make an earth whereon these may dwell." (Abraham 3:24.)

Then our Father said these important words about the experience his children would have on this earth: "And we will prove them herewith, to see if they will do all things whatsoever the Lord their God shall command them." (Abraham 3:25.)

Note those words, "we will prove them herewith." This suggests a test, which we who are going through the mortal experience will certainly agree is the case. The proving, as we have learned from our own experience, comes in many forms. Part of it comes through pain and suffering and anguish that come from the normal processes of living—illness, injury, accidents, death. At other times the proving may come through our own mistakes and transgressions and the pain that comes from them. Still other kinds of proving arise out of the love we have in many of our relationships and the pain that comes when those relationships are damaged or terminated by death. Additional proving comes from within us as we deal with inner pain resulting from our own misreading of reality or lack of understanding about ourselves or our place in the larger scheme of things. All of these kinds of "proving" and the pain they could bring were known and understood before we were born, and then a veil was placed to obscure those premortal memories and the knowledge we had.

The scriptures tell us that mortality began with the fall of Adam and Eve, when death and decay, pain and imperfection became a part of the experience.

We know through modern revelation that we "will be punished for [our] own sins, and not for Adam's transgression."

(Articles of Faith 1:2.) But we also know that through the transgression of Adam and Eve, pain entered the world and became a necessary part of the mortal experience.

As recorded in the third chapter of the book of Moses, our Father in Heaven specifically commanded that our first parents not partake of the tree of the knowledge of good and evil. Satan, approaching the innocent and guileless Eve, asked her to eat of the forbidden fruit and was initially rebuffed. Eve explained that her Father in Heaven had commanded her not to eat of that fruit, and she told the adversary that not only were they not to eat it but they were not even to touch it.

At this point Satan used a clever twisting of the truth to convince Eve that she should take and eat the fruit. He said, "Ye shall not surely die; for God doth know that in the day ye eat thereof, then your eyes shall be opened, and ye shall be as gods, knowing good and evil." (Moses 4:10–11.)

Eve then understood the dilemma she faced. If she and Adam were to grow and learn and progress, they would need to know these things. So Eve consented, took the fruit, and with an incredible display of faith partook of it and gave it also to Adam.

Their first pain occurred with the sinking feeling that they had disobeyed their Father and that things were different now. Then, with eyes opened and with a beginning knowledge of the difference between good and evil, our first parents were confronted by their Father in Heaven, who explained the consequences that would now come upon them and their children through this transgression. To Eve he said, "I will greatly multiply thy sorrow and thy conception. In sorrow thou shalt bring forth children." To Adam he said, "Cursed shall be the ground for thy sake; in sorrow shalt thou eat of it all the days of thy life. Thorns also, and thistles shall it bring forth to thee, and . . . by the sweat of thy face shalt thou eat bread, until thou shalt return unto the ground." (Moses 4:22–25.)

When we read or hear these familiar words, we sometimes overlook what the Lord was really saying. He was indicating to Adam and Eve that mortal life would be painful, and that they would be subject to the great law of opposites we talked about in chapter 2 and that Father Lehi taught in 2 Nephi 2:11: "It must needs be that there is an opposition in all things. If not so, . . . righteousness could not be brought to pass, neither wickedness, neither holiness nor misery, neither good nor bad." Thus, we live in a world of opposites: light or darkness, health or sickness, growth or decline, sweetness or bitterness, joy or anguish, and all the gradations between those extremes.

Without these and other sets of opposites, there would be no way to learn, because we come to understand each by also knowing or experiencing its opposite. Even our senses require opposites to discern what exists out there in the world. That's why we have difficulty seeing in the dark when there is no light, or why we make jokes about a blank piece of paper representing "a polar bear in a snowstorm." Variations in pitch make it possible for us to discern different sounds and words instead of hearing one monotonous tone. As I've thought about these things, I'm amazed at the profound truth Lehi taught his son Jacob, a truth so fundamental to earth life that we almost don't realize that it exists or how it pervades everything.

Isn't it interesting that many of these opposites are exemplified by the characters and attributes of the two sons of God who contended with each other for the privilege of implementing a plan to bring all of us through the mortal experience. We can list many of those diametrically opposed attributes in two columns:

Jesus Christ	*Satan*
Symbolized by light	Symbolized by darkness
Righteous	Evil
Seeks our eternal life	Seeks our death
Builds	Destroys
Loves	Hates
Gives	Takes
Teaches truth	Teaches falsehood
Empowers	Controls
Wants us to be humble	Wants us to be prideful
Wants us to have joy	Wants us to be miserable

Mormon said it well when he gave us the test for knowing what is of God and what is of the adversary: "I show unto you the way to judge; for every thing which inviteth to do good, and to persuade to believe in Christ, is sent forth by the power and gift of Christ; wherefore ye may know with a perfect knowledge it is of God. But whatsoever thing persuadeth men to do evil, and believe not in Christ, and deny him, and serve not God, then ye may know with a perfect knowledge it is of the devil." (Moroni 7: 16–17.)

So now here we are on earth, surrounded by people and things that are grouped and delineated by opposites. In many cases, especially in the natural world, opposites are not necessarily good or bad, they just are, such as hot and cold. But in the realm of human relations, the opposites are often grouped along the spectrum between actions that produce happiness and fulfillment and those that produce pain and sorrow. The important thing to remember in dealing with these opposites, including the pain and sorrow side of the equation, is that they are a necessary part of the mortal experience that help us to learn and grow. And with the road map of the scriptures and the gospel of Jesus Christ, we can learn many of the important choices that will bring us true happiness without having to experience the painful opposite. Using the truths of the gospel as our sure compass will bring us safely through mortality to our destination of eternal life with a loving Father in Heaven and his Beloved Son and our Elder Brother, Jesus Christ.

PAIN HELPS US TO BE HUMBLE

One of the primary purposes of pain in our lives is to help us become humble, and much of our spiritual pain comes from our weaknesses. As the Lord revealed to Moroni, "I give unto men weakness that they may be humble; and my grace is sufficient for all men that humble themselves before me; for if they humble themselves before me, and have faith in me, then will I make weak things become strong unto them." (Ether 12:27.) We don't always need to experience pain in order to achieve humility, but sometimes pain compels us to recognize our weaknesses and humble ourselves before God.

Humility is an interesting word to try to define. It is also a rather elusive character trait, both in terms of obtaining it and holding onto it. It's been said that the moment you say you are humble, you no longer are, and I think there is much truth in that statement.

Benjamin Franklin, a wise and certainly confident member of that talented group we call the Founding Fathers of the United States of America, was honest enough to admit that being humble was not easy for him. When he was twenty-two years old, he identified a set of twelve "virtues" or values that he hoped to espouse and exemplify in his life. These included temperance, silence, order, resolution, frugality, industry, sincerity, justice, moderation, cleanliness, tranquility, and chastity, and he developed a brief description for each of them.

Franklin took his list to a Quaker friend and asked his opinion of them. The friend looked at them and informed Franklin that he had forgotten one: humility. In his autobiography Benjamin Franklin wrote, "He kindly inform'd me that I was generally thought proud; that my Pride show'd itself frequently in Conversation; that I was not content with being in the right when discussing any Point, but was overbearing & rather insolent; of which he convinced me by mentioning several instances." So Franklin added a thirteenth virtue—humility.

Late in his life, Franklin took stock of how well he'd done in acquiring or maintaining the virtues he sought to incorporate in his life. One that seemed to have escaped him for the most part was the one his friend suggested he add to his list. Of humility, Franklin wrote with typical candor, "I cannot boast of much Success in acquiring the *Reality* of this virtue; but I had a good deal with regard to the *Appearance* of it."

I'll have to admit that too often in my life I have not been particularly humble, although perhaps I had the opposite of Franklin's experience with it—I think I was actually more successful in acquiring some of the *reality* of it while not doing as well with the *appearance* of humility.

I can vividly recall, when I was a young man preparing for my mission, the day I received my call in the mail from President David O. McKay. It was an exciting time for me as friends and others came to know that Hyrum Smith was going to London, England, on his mission. Upon hearing of my call, a good number of my friends made it a point to say, "Well Hyrum, you are going on a mission, so I guess you are going to have to get humble now."

After hearing this fifteen or twenty times, I started to get a bit of a complex. Enough people referred to my lack of humility that I began to realize I didn't really exhibit the characteristics of one who had humility, nor had I ever bothered to think about the need for humility. This really bothered me, so I went to a number of people whose judgment I respected and asked them to define humility for me. I got the usual answers you would probably hear from anyone who had made a cursory examination of the subject: "Well, humility is not being proud." "It is not being lifted up." "It is not being boisterous or loud." "It is being teachable." I had heard most of these responses before.

These definitions were all right but didn't seem to get to the root of the matter. Many of them seemed to emphasize what humility is *not* rather than what it is. Then I read a talk by Spencer W. Kimball, who was at the time a member of the Quorum of the Twelve. In his talk he said that humility was something you can never recognize in yourself. Well, reading that created a serious dilemma in my mind. If humility was something I needed to acquire to serve well in the mission field, how would I ever know when I had it if I could never recognize it in myself? This perceived shortcoming caused me a good deal of thought over the next several months as I prepared to serve my mission, but I wasn't able to fully resolve my dilemma before I departed for England.

Several months into my mission, I found myself in the

home of a British Saint by the name of Derek Hill. Derek was an English policeman—a "bobby"—who had just lost his wife a few weeks earlier to a debilitating disease. As I had observed Brother Hill over the few weeks I had known him, he seemed to exhibit the characteristics you would associate with someone who had humility. And so, one evening while we were in his home, I asked him, "Derek, how would you define this thing called humility?"

Brother Hill paused for several moments. Then he looked me straight in the eye and said words that set off tolling bells in my mind, because finally this was the answer I had been searching for: "Elder Smith, *humility is the realization of our total dependence on God.*"

I wish I could tell you the impact of those words, the spirit in which they were uttered, and the effect they had on me. It was one of the major "aha's" I have experienced in this life. Something deep within my soul said, *Well, of course that is what humility is.* The instant we are able to totally acknowledge, accept, and believe that everything we have, are, or ever will be is a gift from God, then humility begins to silently and inconspicuously creep into our hearts. And we will never recognize it, because we are too busy being grateful for the fact that we depend totally, solely, and completely on our Father in Heaven and the blessings he pours out upon us. Then the characteristics of humility begin to be evident, and other people see what we never see in ourselves. This has become my answer to anyone who is searching for the real definition of humility.

So forty years ago, tutored by a humble Englishman in that humble English home, I realized that humility was something I could go after, something I could hope to acquire.

Being genetically disposed toward action, I mounted a quest to discover and realize my total and complete dependence on my Father in Heaven. It has taken many years, many experiences where I was compelled to be humble, and much pain and anguish, but I have come to finally understand the truth and profound nature of Derek Hill's definition of humility. And as I read the scriptures now and have studied them since that time in England many years ago, every time I see the word *humility* or read a description of a great leader like Moroni, Nephi, or Paul, those words of the Lord's humble servant Derek Hill come ringing back. *Humility is the realization of our total dependence on God.*

Pain Helps Us to Have a "Broken Heart and a Contrite Spirit"

The most anguishing kind of pain often comes self-inflicted, by way of major transgression of the Lord's commandments. It is a pain felt when we recognize the gulf that exists between what the Lord has commanded us to do and what we are actually doing. This kind of heavy-duty pain— weighing upon our spirits like lead, piercing us to the soul with self-doubt and self-loathing—is there not just to make us feel remorseful about what we have done. It also serves an important function in the process of repentance.

Let's talk about the gospel the missionaries are taking to the world. If someone were to ask me where they could find the most complete and concise scripture that defines the gospel, I would take them to the second chapter of 2 Nephi and have them read verses 6, 7, and 8. Here is a wonderful description of what the plan of salvation is really all about, and why the Lord has made it so important to take this message to all the world.

In verse 6 we read, "Redemption cometh in and through the Holy Messiah; for he is full of grace and truth." So the first thing that we learn is where redemption comes from. It comes from Jesus Christ, the Holy Messiah. Why? Because he is full of grace and truth.

Now read verse 7. "Behold he [the Savior] offereth himself a sacrifice for sin, to answer the ends of the law, unto all those who have a broken heart and a contrite spirit; and unto none else can the ends of the law be answered." In this brief verse we are taught many powerful things.

We first learn about justice and justification. No unclean thing can enter the presence of God. If a sin occurs, justice requires that the sin be repaid. Our Savior, recognizing that fact, had to come up with a way for sins to be paid for, for the demands of justice to be met. And so we read in the very first line of verse 7 that the Holy Messiah offered himself a sacrifice for sin "to answer the ends of the law." That is the clearest, briefest, most wonderful statement I have ever read describing what Jesus Christ's sacrifice and the doctrine of justification is all about.

Even more powerful than this principle is what we learn in the next line about whom this sacrifice was made for: "*all those who have a broken heart and a contrite spirit.*" I talk about this fundamental principle at other places in this book because the necessity of having a broken heart and a contrite spirit is a central theme of this book and part of the reason why I felt compelled to write it. The one thing that will bring all of the blessings of the universe is the ability to develop and have a broken heart and a contrite spirit.

There is one final verse in this scriptural sequence we should not leave out. Verse 8 states, "Wherefore, how great the importance to make these things known unto the inhabitants of the earth."

Now, to briefly summarize what has been presented in verses 6, 7, and 8 of 2 Nephi, chapter 2:

- What is so important for the world to know? That redemption cometh in and through the Holy Messiah.
- Why did the Savior do this? Because he is full of grace and truth.
- For what purpose was it done? To answer the ends of the law.
- And for whom was it done? Only for those who have a broken heart and contrite spirit.

So we discover that this magnificent sacrifice the Lord undertook on our behalf is only for those who have a broken heart and a contrite spirit. The last line of verse 7 stipulates, "and unto none else can the ends of the law be answered." That is a very sobering statement. It means that if we don't achieve and internalize this state of a broken heart and contrite spirit, the Savior's atonement and sacrifice will not cover our sins. We will be on our own when we move into the next world.

When the judgment day comes, rather than having the Savior as our advocate with the Father, we will be standing at the judgment bar alone. Our Father is going to ask us some very pointed questions, and we will discover that we are not capable of paying for our sins ourselves. We may find ourselves turned away at that point, or at least given to know that we still have a long way to go on the road of eternal progression to be where we should have been at that point of the journey.

This is only my opinion, but I believe that when we stand before the Father, we will need the Savior as our advocate before we are allowed into the kingdom and glory of our Father in Heaven.

So what does it mean to have a broken heart and a contrite spirit? It doesn't mean that our heart and spirit have been "broken," in the sense we see in films and read in literature, when through physical torture or beating a person is brought to a point where, cowering, he or she is ready to confess or is coerced into submission. That is the way things probably would have worked if Lucifer were in charge of running the world, in accordance with his "surely I will save everyone" campaign.

The broken heart and contrite spirit the Savior talks about are actually evidence of a deeper level of humility, one that comes when we know without a doubt how utterly dependent we are on the Lord and his mercy. Redemption through the Atonement does not come about by force and compulsion on his part, but rather by love and patience. On our part, this condition comes when we recognize that we have great need of his intercession in our behalf, when we want to return to him and our Father more than anything else, and when we realize that we have absolutely no chance of doing it alone.

A broken heart and contrite spirit can come about through the intense pain and anguish of repentance when we have transgressed, but that isn't the only way we can come to this state. Having a broken heart and a contrite spirit can also be the result of the process of sanctification, when we find ourselves with no desire for evil or transgression, when we have felt the love the Savior and our Father in Heaven have for us, and when we desire above all else to regain their presence and again behold their faces. Whether we arrive at the broken heart and contrite spirit in the depths of despair or in a state of gratitude and joy as we find ourselves drawing closer to sanctification, it will be a necessary condition for us if we are to receive eternal life.

There is much deep water that could be explored in answering the paradoxical question of why pain is a part of the Lord's plan of happiness, and we have only touched the surface. But please know that pain and suffering came upon all as a result of the Fall, and it is a "given" in the mortal phase of our eternal lives. We knew that pain would be part of the plan, and just as Adam and Eve chose, so we chose to accept sorrow, hardships, death, and pain. But know as well that those negative experiences are not in the plan capriciously or without larger purpose. As we have seen, pain is a necessary part of how we come to differentiate the good from the evil. It helps us learn what is true and real and good, through our experiences in dealing with the "opposition in all things" that Father Lehi spoke about. Pain provides us with the opportunity for spiritual growth. It helps us attain humility, and it helps us realize our complete dependence on God. While we may not seek or want pain, we must learn to appreciate its presence in our lives and the important role it plays in our personal eternal progression.

CHAPTER 4

KNOW WHO YOU REALLY ARE

This above all: to thine own self be true,
And it must follow, as the night the day,
Thou canst not then be false to any man.

—William Shakespeare

Personality is born out of pain. It is the fire shut up in the flint.

—J. B. Yeats

In the previous chapter we explored the role of pain as part of the plan of mortality. Only through pain and its resulting darkness can we fully appreciate the joy of the light. Yet, sometimes the pain can be so debilitating and overwhelming that it's easy to get discouraged and want to throw in the towel.

In order to fully avail yourself of the great plan of happiness that has been provided to enable us to live again with our Father in Heaven and his Beloved Son, Jesus Christ, you must come to know who you really are: a child of divine parents, a part of a royal family, endowed with the capacity to make it through the mortal testing period and return to your heavenly home. This is the most valuable knowledge you can have for your journey here on earth.

An essential step in knowing who you really are is to come to know for yourself that all this stuff about a plan—a Heavenly Father, a Savior, a pre- and post-earth life, and a living prophet through whom this knowledge has been given—is true. That sure knowledge and testimony is the key that unlocks the workings of the plan for you as a son or daughter of God. And it is the key to unlocking the courage required to face and overcome the pain of this mortal experience.

Knowing for Yourself

Although I was born in Utah, my family moved to Hawaii when I was three years old, and I lived in Honolulu until I was eighteen. During my junior year in high school, my father, a professor of speech at the University of Hawaii, exchanged jobs and houses with a professor from New York University. So I found myself in New York City, living on Long Island, and attending a large New York City high school. It was an interesting cultural shock, by the way, moving from a Honolulu high school of three hundred students to a New York City school of forty-five hundred students!

During that year I became acquainted with a young man by the name of Arthur Gaines. He was a year older than I was. For some reason, we hit it off and became close friends. At the end of my junior year, when it came time for us to leave New York and return to Honolulu, I had become so enamored with the city and had such a close friendship with Artie that I prevailed on my parents to allow me to stay in New York for that summer and live with the Gaines family. They relented, and my family proceeded to travel across the country through Salt Lake City on their way back to Hawaii.

That summer was a changing point in my life for a number

of reasons. Artie and his family were not members of the Church, and because I had no easy way to get to the nearest LDS congregation, it wasn't convenient for me to go to church that summer. So I didn't.

We had wonderful jobs working for the Douglaston Yacht Club on Little Neck Bay, which juts in from Long Island Sound. Our job was to drive a very fancy launch from the pier out into the bay and drop people off at their luxurious yachts. On weekends, we would sometimes crew for people on their yachts, which was a great deal of fun. As a result of these wonderful jobs, we became rather full of ourselves and were pretty sure that we were the greatest thing since sliced bread.

We would jog to and from work each day. One evening as we were jogging home from the pier, we started to discuss religion. Artie proceeded to tell me all about his church. I can't remember which religion he described, but he described it in some detail.

As we jogged into his yard, he said an interesting thing: "You know, Hyrum, religion is great for little kids and old folks. But we don't need it, right?"

I remember trying not to respond to that. As we walked into his home, close to midnight, he said, "You're a Mormon, right?"

I responded that I was. He asked me to tell him about the Mormons. At this point, we were in his room. I proceeded to take the next six or eight minutes to tell him all I could remember about the Church. As I began to tell him the story, I found myself becoming uncomfortable. In fact, I began to sweat, realizing that I had launched into a story that I was now going to have to complete. Thinking back, this is how my story must have sounded to Artie Gaines that night:

"Well, Artie, there was this kid in upstate New York." And here we were, living in New York. "He lived in a little town with a lot of churches. Everyone wanted him to join his or her church. He was really confused and didn't know what he should do. One day he was reading in his father's Bible, in the book of James, as I recall. The Bible said that if you want to know about this kind of stuff, you ought to pray about it. So this kid decided to go out into the forest near his father's farm and give it a shot. One morning, he goes out into this forest." At this point, I found myself very uncomfortable. "This kid kneels down and starts to pray. While he is praying, this big light appears in the forest. He looks up into the light and sees two people standing in the light." I stopped and looked at Artie. His eyes were as big as saucers.

At this point, he immediately interrupted me and said, "Is that right? Who was it?"

I said, "Well, actually, it was God and Christ."

He said, "Is that right? You mean they have been to New York?"

You know, I had never quite thought about it like that before. I said, "Yes, I guess they have."

I got off that story as quickly as possible because I could see he was clearly blown away by it. I said some things about pioneers and Utah and ended my story. When I finished the story, Arthur's eyes had not gotten any smaller. He looked at me in wild disbelief and said words I will never forget. The words came in the form of a question: "Hyrum, do you really believe all that?"

I remember what my conditioned response to that question was, or what I wanted it to be. I wanted to be able to say, "Of course I believe that. I, Hyrum Smith, know that is true."

But because of the relationship I had with Artie Gaines, I was *not* able to say that. He was almost like a brother to me. I looked him in the eye that night and said, "Well, Artie, as a matter of fact, no one ever asked me that before. To be honest with you, I don't know for sure for myself that it is true. I know my family believes it. They have believed it for a long time. But, as for me, I guess I'm not really sure."

Then his eyes went back to their normal size. He said, "Boy, I'm sure glad. That's the wildest story I've ever heard." He then rolled over and went to sleep.

I rolled over that night and reviewed my thoughts and listened to myself tell that story again: a fourteen-year-old boy, in upstate New York (not all that far from where I was), light in the forest, people standing in the light. I said to myself, "Hyrum, that is a heavy story."

I woke up the next morning wanting to know if it was true more than I had ever wanted to know anything else in my life. I found myself thinking, *You know, Hyrum, there are only two possibilities. Either it happened or it didn't happen. And if it didn't happen, your family has been messed up for a very long time.*

On the other hand, I found myself thinking, *But you know, if it did happen, it is the most important event that has taken place on this planet since the Savior came the first time.* I then embarked on a personal quest to find out whether that story I had told Artie Gaines was true. I won't tell you how long it took. I think it is different for everyone, as far as the length of time needed to really know.

A couple of years later I felt good enough about the reality of that story that I decided to go on a mission. I arrived in London, England, in March 1963. My mission president was

Elder Marion D. Hanks, who in my mind is one of the greatest teachers on earth. He was a young General Authority at that time and was serving as president of the British Mission. I will never forget the day I walked into his office for my first interview after having just come off the airplane from the States. He had me sit down, looked me steadily in the eye, and asked me this question: "Elder Smith, have you read the Book of Mormon all the way through, cover to cover, for yourself?"

My response to that question was, "Well, sort of. I went to seminary, you know."

He said, "You haven't answered my question. I want to know if you have read the Book of Mormon for yourself, cover to cover, all the way through."

I then looked my new mission president in the eye and decided that, as it was in my experience with Artie Gaines, it was time to be honest. I said, "No, as a matter of fact, President Hanks, I have not done that for myself."

He then said, "Elder Smith, I don't want to see you again for twenty-nine days. In that period of time, I want you to read the Book of Mormon twice. Then, apply the test you will read about in the book of Moroni. Do you have any questions?"

I had no questions. That was my initial interview with President Marion D. Hanks.

I took that assignment seriously. I went to my area, which was just north of London in Edgeware, Middlesex, and began to read the Book of Mormon. I am not a fast reader. Sandwiching reading into all the little moments between appointments and other missionary work, it took me the full twenty-nine days to finish the assignment. In fact, I don't remember sleeping much during that last week. But I did read the book—twice.

As I worked my way through the Book of Mormon, I had many experiences in which I realized by some strange, certain, inner feeling that what I was reading was true. Not only did I realize that what I was reading was true but also that somehow I had read that information or been taught that information before. That was not only an exciting feeling; it was a chilling feeling as well. I had hundreds of "aha's" and "wows" as I went through that experience. Something deep in my center, my core, was saying to me, "I knew this before. This is true, Hyrum Smith. What you are reading is true."

Twenty-nine days later, I walked back into the office of President Marion D. Hanks a changed young man. He didn't have to ask me whether or not I had read the book twice. He could tell by looking at me. The interview was very different this time. We talked about the reality of the restoration of the gospel and the fact that a young boy did see two personages standing in the light in his father's forest in upstate New York in 1820.

From the time of my experience with Artie Gaines in New York to my experience with the Book of Mormon in suburban London, less than three years had elapsed. Yet, motivated by Artie's challenge to my complacently held beliefs, and through the literal fulfillment to me as a missionary of Moroni's promise, I had learned two of the most important and life-governing natural laws.

First, I came to know that the Holy Ghost is real, and that, as promised by Moroni, "by the power of the Holy Ghost [we] may know the truth of all things." (Moroni 10:5.)

Second, I came to understand that learning how to know

what is true—and conversely, what is not—is one of the most important skills we must have if we are to navigate the rocky shoals of earth life and successfully return to our Father in Heaven.

After I was spiritually mature enough to understand the process and transformation I had gone through in finding out for myself, I realized I had followed the blueprint described in the fifth chapter of Alma on how testimonies of God, Jesus Christ, and the restoration of the gospel are obtained. The simple formula has not changed for several thousand years: "Do ye not suppose that I know of these things myself? Behold, I testify unto you that I do know that these things whereof I have spoken are true. And how do ye suppose that I know of their surety? Behold, I say unto you they are made known unto me by the Holy Spirit of God. Behold, *I have fasted and prayed many days* that I might know these things of myself. And now I do know of myself that they are true; for the Lord God hath made them manifest unto me by his Holy Spirit." (Alma 5:45–46.)

Gaining such knowledge requires a lot of study, a lot of fasting, and a great deal of prayer. When we are willing to do those three things, the Spirit can work in us. When we follow the blueprint and come to know the gospel really is true, when the Holy Spirit confirms to our souls that the things we have been taught are real and come from our Heavenly Father, we then have the most important knowledge it is possible to obtain in this life.

KNOWING WHO YOU REALLY ARE

Through that fantastic experience I described to Artie Gaines about heavenly personages appearing to a young boy in a grove of trees, we now have knowledge—revealed by God to that young boy—of who we really are and what we can become. It is a lofty view of men and women, lifting our souls far beyond the despair of the world's limited understanding of such things. The implications of the "merciful plan of the great Creator" outlined in chapter 2 are simple and awe-inspiring in their power to motivate us. A poem I have sometimes heard quoted in sacrament meeting talks describes it well:

> *I am a child of royal birth.*
> *My Father is King of heaven and earth.*
> *My spirit came from courts on high,*
> *A child beloved, a prince am I.*
> —Anna Johnson

A loving Father did not send us to earth empty-handed and clueless. He has revealed a road map showing the way back—the gospel of Jesus Christ—brought to us by his own Beloved Son and the prophets he sent to share that knowledge with the world. And I believe that our Heavenly Father sent each of us to earth with our own spiritual endowment of knowledge, locked away deep within us, to be unlocked by the power of the Holy Ghost and called to our remembrance at times when we need that inner knowledge.

Just as each of us is different and unique and our physical bodies have a completely different genetic makeup, I believe that our spiritual endowment is unique, imprinted with our own spiritual DNA. I like to think of our spiritual DNA as the genetic heritage given us as spirit children of God, our Father in Heaven. Just as our physical DNA contains all of the instructions and information needed to create our bodies and enable them to function, so I believe that our spiritual DNA contains all the instructions and knowledge we will need to successfully fulfill our mortal existence and return to our Heavenly Father.

This inner spiritual endowment lies at the center of our being, in what my friend and poet Stan Bronson has called the "uttermost chambers of the heart." I believe that locked within those deepest chambers is this great wealth of knowledge that we learned in the "courts on high" during our premortal existence. Although we don't have the keys to unlock those secret chambers and reveal their knowledge, the Holy Ghost does. Jesus taught his disciples that the Holy Ghost "shall teach you all things, and bring all things to your remembrance, whatsoever I have said unto you." (John 14:26.) And I believe that "all things" includes not just what we've learned from Jesus in mortality but also what he taught us in the realms before we came here. I believe that's why we have "déjà vu" experiences—those times when it seems like we've seen or done things before but can't place where or when. And the Savior's promise of remembrance also helps explain those moments when we feel, in the Prophet Joseph Smith's words, "pure knowledge flowing into us"—sudden flashes of inspiration, of knowing things we didn't know before but of which we instantly have a certain and pure knowledge.

The Holy Ghost, then, holds the key to unlocking those uttermost chambers of the heart, on those occasions when we need the eternal knowledge those chambers contain. As we humble ourselves and seek his help, he will open these inner chambers and bring back to our remembrance sacred knowledge that will help us make our way back home. In the process of unlocking the uttermost chambers of our hearts, we will come to know who we really are, what gifts and talents the Lord gave us in that heavenly endowment, and what he expects us to do with them.

It's important to remember that the gifts and talents he gave you, and what he expects of you, will be different from what they will be for me, or anyone else for that matter. We are each one of a kind, and the Lord expects us, in the phrasing of a popular U.S. Army recruiting slogan from a few years ago, to "be all that [we] can be."

Jerry Pulsipher, a friend, colleague, and fellow British missionary, had the opportunity to attend a special meeting in London in 1961 where President David O. McKay spoke to the assembled missionaries and emphasized this very point. In Jerry's words, "Among other things, President McKay counseled the missionaries concerning what was becoming an increasing tendency among young people in the 1960s to 'do their own thing.' While cautioning against the rebellious attitudes prevalent among many at that time, President McKay said, 'It's all right to be yourself. But you should *not only be yourself, but be that perfectly.*'" That counsel has stayed with and guided Jerry through his life since, and he has had opportunities to serve in and out of the Church in ways that reflect his particular mix of personality, abilities, interests, and talents—many of which are part of that spiritual DNA he brought to earth with him.

It is my belief that the Lord expects that of all of us. We need to strive to truly be all that we can be. We don't need to, and shouldn't, compare ourselves with others and wish we could be this person or that person. You don't have their spiritual endowment, and they don't have yours. When each of us fully realizes that eternal truth, believes it, and acts on it, then we will find that the Holy Ghost may begin to unlock those inner chambers. Then, and only then, will the Holy Ghost help us use the treasures within to fulfill the purposes the Lord has for us.

For active Latter-day Saints, the scriptures also provide glimpses of who we are in a very special and humbling sense. To Father Abraham thousands of years ago, the Lord gave a powerful and revealing vision: "The Lord had shown unto me, Abraham, the intelligences that were organized before the world was; and among all these there were many of the noble and great ones; and God saw these souls that they were good, and he stood in the midst of them, and he said: These I will make my rulers; for he stood among those that were spirits, . . . and he said unto me: Abraham, thou art one of them; thou wast chosen before thou wast born." (Abraham 3:22–23.)

I believe that all of us were at that great council, and that many were numbered among the "noble and great ones." The Prophet Joseph Smith taught, "Every man [and woman] who has a calling to minister to the inhabitants of the world was ordained to that very purpose in the Grand Council of heaven before this world was." (*Teachings of the Prophet Joseph Smith*, selected and arranged by Joseph Fielding Smith [Salt Lake City: Deseret Book, 1976], 365.)

It's important to remember that being "noble and great" and possibly even a "ruler" does not give any of us some kind of exalted status. Jesus himself taught through example that the master is the servant of all, and committed Latter-day Saints rejoice and find fulfillment in being servants of the true Master. Still, I hope you glimpse through these revealed words not only that you are a son or daughter of God, as all who come to earth are, but also that you are a member of the

Royal Family. And if you have been called to serve our Father and God in this life, you can be sure that he has equipped you with everything you need to serve well and return with honor.

So it's important that you remember who you are in this eternal sense. You're not just a biological accident or a meaningless bit of foam on a wave in the cosmos but a son or daughter of a Heavenly Father who loves you, and who did not send you here without a compass, a map, or instructions on how to return to him. Those items are found both in the gospel, which has been given us by Jesus Christ and his appointed prophets, and also in the individualized treasures locked inside those uttermost chambers of your heart.

Your own personal spiritual endowment will help you understand who you really are and what you should be doing here on earth, but the map and printed guide have been pro vided by the Lord through the ministry of his Beloved Son and through the prophets he has appointed throughout history to help show his sons and daughters the way. This road map and printed guide are found in the scriptures and in the recorded teachings of the Lord's prophets, and they constitute a sure guide through the inevitable painful experiences that will in the end bring you home to a loving Father in Heaven. I like the words of C. S. Lewis describing that heavenly homecoming, as quoted by Elder Neal A. Maxwell in his book *A Time to Choose* ([Salt Lake City: Deseret Book, 1972], 22): "We shall of course be very muddy and tattered children by the time we reach home. But the bathrooms are all ready, the towels put out, and the clean clothes in the airing cupboard." (*Letters of C. S. Lewis,* ed. W. H. Lewis; rev. and enlarged edition, edited by Walter Hooper [New York: Harcourt Brace & Co., 1993], 365.)

CHAPTER 5

"IF THOU ENDURE IT WELL"

My son, peace be unto thy soul; thine adversity and thine afflictions shall be but a small moment; and then, if thou endure it well, God shall exalt thee on high; thou shalt triumph over all thy foes.
—Doctrine and Covenants 121:7–8

God, give us the serenity to accept what cannot be changed, the courage to change what should be changed, and the wisdom to distinguish one from the other.

—Reinhold Neibuhr

When I went on my mission in 1963 to London, England, my family was living on Long Island, just outside New York City. I flew to Salt Lake City to go through the mission training experience that was offered in what was called the Mission Home near Temple Square. (This was several years before the Missionary Training Center had been developed in Provo.) At the conclusion of my training I flew with eight other missionaries back to New York, there to transfer to a flight that would take us to London. It turned out that we had about a five-hour layover between planes. Because my family's home was a relatively short drive from the airport, I had the opportunity to visit with my father and mother before we departed for London.

Just before I boarded the plane that day to leave for my mission field, my father gave me a hug, and he said two very interesting things. First, he said, "Hyrum, remember, while you are on your mission, *the sorrows will far outnumber the joys, but the joys will far outweigh the sorrows.*" Then he told me, "We may not meet again in this life. No one knows. But," he continued, "serve your mission with honor."

I thought a lot about that statement as we flew across the Atlantic. *The sorrows will far* outnumber *the joys, but the joys will far* outweigh *the sorrows.* That statement would turn out to be prophetic not only about my missionary experience but also about my entire life. The tough, hard experiences will most likely outnumber the good ones in our lives, but hopefully we forget the difficult ones because the really sweet, spiritual, wonderful experiences the Lord provides do far outweigh the bad experiences.

My father's other statement—we might not meet again in this life—turned out to be prophetic as well. I was not prepared for the reality that his prophecy would be fulfilled quite so soon after he uttered those words.

In August 1964 I was sitting in the office of the West European Mission home. I had been assigned as an assistant to Elder Mark E. Petersen, a member of the Quorum of the Twelve, who was living in England at the time, presiding over the affairs of all the West European missions, my own included. I had become quite close to Elder Petersen. Living in his home in for eight months and watching this servant of the Lord daily was one of the great experiences of my life. He was and remains for me one of the truly noble and great ones.

As I was sitting in my office this particular evening, I had an overpowering impression that I needed to communicate to my father how much I loved and appreciated all he had done in my life. The impression was so powerful that I got up from my desk and told my companion, Elder Homer, that we needed to go into town and buy an audio tape so I could send my father an expression of my love for him. Elder Homer got his stuff, and we drove into Leatherhead, a little town not far from the mission home, about twenty miles south of London, where I purchased a reel-to-reel tape. We didn't have cassette tapes in those days, and it was burdensome to use the larger tape recorders that were almost like threading a movie projector.

When we got back I cloistered myself in my room, turned on the recorder, and filled the entire reel of tape, more than half an hour of speaking. I shared with my father my gratitude for all the things he had done for me and the impact he'd had on my life. I concluded by telling him that I had finally learned to love and appreciate Shakespeare.

Now, prior to my mission I couldn't stand Shakespeare. My father was a noted professor of speech and a world-renowned speaker in the United States at the time, and Shakespeare was one of his heroes. In his lifetime, my father had performed in several plays, Shakespeare's being among them. Still, I wanted nothing to do with Shakespeare when I was at home. My rapid conversion to Shakespeare was thanks to Elder Marion D. Hanks, my mission president, another mentor and spiritual giant who also had a huge impact in my life. On one occasion Elder Hanks insisted that we go to the Aldwych Theatre in London, and he ordered us to see Shakespearean plays on P-days when we had the chance.

When I saw Shakespeare done well, I came to love the language he employed, to love Shakespeare's words and well-expressed thoughts. I shared my newfound appreciation with my father on the tape, put the tape in the mail, and promptly forgot about it.

On the morning of August 25 my companion and I were at church at the Epson Ward, a few miles from where we lived. During the meeting a gentleman came in and said there was a phone call for me. I went into the lobby of the ward house and found that my mother was on the phone. She was quite distraught, and she shared with me the unexpected news that my father had passed away suddenly of a heart attack the day before. Of course, I was stunned by this news. My mother said that the family was all in Salt Lake City for the wedding of my sister Lynne and that the funeral would be held in a few days. She then told me that she would very much like me to come home for the funeral.

I hung up the phone and grabbed my companion, and we drove back to the West European mission home. I began to make preparations for an unanticipated trip back to the United States so I could be present for my father's funeral. We hadn't been home more than fifteen minutes when the phone rang. I picked it up and heard the voice of Elder Harold B. Lee of the Quorum of the Twelve. Elder Lee had been a close friend of my father's, and he said, "Elder Smith, are you preparing to come home for your father's funeral?"

My response was, "Yes, sir, I am."

His response was not what I expected: "Elder Smith, you stay right where you are. Your father would not want you to come home for his funeral. You are there on a mission in the

Lord's service. You stay there and complete your mission. Do you have any questions?"

I said, "No, sir, I have no questions." He said, "Very fine," and then he hung up. End of conversation. That was my one experience with Elder Harold B. Lee.

Well, it was clear that I wasn't going to be going home for the funeral. Being so instructed so soon upon the heels of my mother's unexpected news just added to the pain I felt. Even so, I felt a certain peace about what Elder Lee had counseled. And my mother had said one thing that, in the midst of the pain of dealing with the news about my father's passing, actually caused me a great deal of joy. She had said, "You will be interested to know that the night before he died, your father listened to the tape you sent to him from England." She related that he had wept when he listened to it, particularly the part when he discovered that I had finally learned to know and love Shakespeare.

Now, after Elder Lee's call, I got goose bumps when I thought about that, because somehow the Spirit had gotten through to me that expressing love and gratitude to my father was something I needed to do immediately. That has given me great peace over the years as I have thought back about that event.

The next thing that happened that memorable Sunday I will never forget. Elder Petersen was in France at a district conference. He was generally gone on weekends, and we rarely traveled with him when he went to these conferences. On this particular weekend, he had taken his wife, and they were traveling in France alone.

In the eight months I had served as Elder Petersen's assistant, he had never called the mission home once he left to go to a mission conference. He usually left on a Friday night or Saturday morning and got back late Sunday night or Monday morning, but he would never call us to check in or see how we were doing. He was always occupied with interviews or calling new stake presidents or district presidents. He just never called.

So I was surprised when, a few minutes after the call came from Elder Lee, the phone rang again. It was Elder Mark E. Petersen calling from France. He said, "Elder Smith, something is wrong. What is it?"

I was stunned by the phone call. I then explained, "Elder Petersen, my father passed away, and my mother called me this morning to tell me. That is what is wrong. I have been instructed by Elder Lee that I am to stay here, in the mission field."

To my shock, really, Elder Petersen said, "I will be home as quickly as I can." He then canceled his scheduled meetings for the rest of the day and made arrangements to come home on the first flight from Paris.

That evening, before Elder Petersen was able to arrive home, we had an appointment to teach a family who lived not far from the mission home. Our discussion was to be on the plan of salvation. Since Elder Petersen was coming home a little earlier than our scheduled appointment, I dispatched my companion to go to the airport to pick up the Petersens, and I found a youth missionary from the Epson Ward who could be my companion for the discussion.

In those days we used flannel boards upon which we placed words and illustrations to teach the various concepts in the discussion. For the plan of salvation discussion, we had on our flannel board an illustration representing the premortal life, a picture representing birth, another picture depicting the mortal experience, and then representations of death, the spirit world, and the three kingdoms that would be our eventual rewards. It was very instructive for an investigator to "see" the eternal process that our journey through this life is a part of.

I later realized that it was not just coincidence I was called upon to teach this particular lesson that night, so soon after having learned that my father had gone through the final phase of the mortal part of that plan. And I found myself teaching that discussion with more power, more understanding, and more empathy than I had ever done before or since. It was a sweet experience.

When I got home from the discussion, I was humbled to see a member of the Quorum of the Twelve standing in the driveway of the mission home waiting for me. As I stepped out of the car he came up and embraced me and told me he loved me. Then he said we needed to talk. We went into his office and visited for nearly five hours. I don't think we went to bed until one or two in the morning.

That visit probably had as much impact on the direction of my young life as any single event that happened before or shortly after. When my father served as patriarch to the Church in the 1940s, and the patriarch still met with the Quorum of the Twelve each week, my father sat next to Mark E. Petersen in those meetings. As a result, Elder Petersen knew my father well. That night he shared with me things about my father that I had never known before. He helped me much better appreciate the man my father was. And he helped me better understand who I was, and some of the things the Lord would expect of me as one of his servants.

I share this whole experience with you because through it

I learned some important lessons about how the Lord helps us deal with the pain and anguish that come unbidden and unwanted. True, the unexpected news of my father's passing sent shock waves through me. But the Lord had not left me to wonder about all the whys and "if onlys" that often accompany unexpected and unwelcome events. Although I did not recognize it at the time, a series of amazing spiritual occurrences unfolded before, during, and after that event. I can clearly see now how the Holy Spirit prompted me, and others, to do certain things that brought me comfort and powerfully influenced my life for good. I still marvel that I was so blessed, and I am doubly grateful that busy servants of the Lord were willing to heed those promptings and bring comfort and understanding to a young man who was still very much a "greenie" when it came to knowing and understanding the eternal plan of our Father in Heaven.

It had all begun with the prophetic counsel my father had given me months before, on the day I boarded that airplane in New York City. Then there was my impression, seemingly for no particular reason at the time, to send a taped message to my father. After my mother's call, there came the impression of Elder Lee to call me and put what was a devastating event into a more eternal perspective by revealing to me through his prophetic inspiration what my father's will was in the matter of my going home for the funeral. This was followed almost immediately by Elder Petersen's impression in France that something was wrong, his call to the mission office, and the subsequent meeting in which he helped me put the events into perspective and ultimately find peace.

As I look at all of those events, I am still amazed at the specific orchestration of people and events that the Holy

Ghost accomplished. I learned the literal truth of my father's statement that the joys of mortality would indeed outweigh the sorrows. I also realized that if we are willing to order our lives so that we can be receptive to those promptings, and then try to be spiritually sensitive enough to recognize them when they come, we will be given the power to deal with whatever pain we are called upon to endure.

I was able to get through the experience of the passing of my father while I served in the mission field not only because of an amazing amount of help from the Lord but also from the love transmitted to me by family, friends, and people like Elder Petersen and Elder Hanks, among many others. These people and these experiences sustained me through a very difficult time. I also realize from my experiences since then that these kinds of promptings and spiritual assurances come to many Latter-day Saints at times of grief and pain and loss.

One such was related to me recently by my colleague Jerry Pulsipher about a special experience he witnessed a couple of years ago while serving as a bishop. This involved the accidental death of a longtime member of his ward, a man much beloved for his long years of service in Scouting and the youth programs of the Church. While he was cutting the grass in a small orchard behind his home, a large tree limb fell on this good brother as he was riding his power mower. No other members of the family were present when this freak accident occurred, and his wife discovered the tragedy when she returned from shopping.

Jerry had been summoned, and he arrived while the police were still there investigating the accident as family members began to arrive. Jerry sought to comfort the shocked and grief-stricken wife and console other members of the family as medical personnel performed the sad duty of removing the body. He then walked back into the orchard to see what had happened. The riding mower was still there, beneath a large fruit tree where the jagged end of a limb could be seen near the top of the tree. The fallen branch still lay across the mower. The medical personnel had told the family that death had apparently come instantly when the heavy branch had struck the man, knocking him to the ground.

"It all seemed so bizarre," Jerry told me. "The tree and the fallen branch looked healthy, and there was no sign of disease or other weakness that would have explained how or why this could have happened. Even more puzzling was the apparent timing of the accident—at the exact moment when the mower passed beneath that tree. A couple of feet in either direction, and this tragedy wouldn't have happened."

Jerry, like the family and gathering neighbors, was at a loss to understand this accident, which took a faithful husband, father, and grandfather several years before he would normally pass on. After visiting with the family, providing what comfort he could, and being assured that the grieving widow was surrounded by family and loved ones who could help, Jerry went home. Before departing, he promised to call later to begin making funeral arrangements and discuss related matters. Telephoning just around sunset, Jerry reached the widow and was surprised to find her in seemingly good spirits. "She told me about an incredible experience that had assured the family that this was not a random, senseless accident," Jerry related. "She said that just before sundown the family had all gathered by the tree, pondering the events that had just occurred. One of the sons had been working at remodeling a house in a nearby neighborhood when the accident happened, and he was having a particularly difficult time. He felt that had he been in tune enough with the Spirit, he surely could have rushed to the accident scene and perhaps saved his father, or at least summoned medical help sooner."

Jerry then told me of an incredible experience this woman related to him. "As they were standing there, one of them noticed a bird—a dove—perched on the jagged end of the tree's limb. The amazing thing was that the dove remained there, even though a dog barked at it and the large family group below could have frightened it away."

According to Jerry, the bird remained on its perch as long as the family stood there, and they felt a great sense of peace about all that had happened. "To this family, the bird was a direct manifestation of the Holy Ghost, sent to provide comfort and peace. As I listened to her account, I thought what an appropriate symbol the Lord had used—the dove, the bird universally associated with peace and love."

Then, after describing to Jerry this special manifestation, the woman continued, "Finally we decided to leave the orchard and go to the patio, where we could talk and visit about everything that had happened. As we moved, the bird left its perch in the tree and flew with us to the patio area. There it landed on a branch in another tree where it remained in full view, watching over us." Then came words that sent shivers up and down Jerry's spine: "In fact, the dove is still here, and I'm looking at it even as we're talking."

Jerry told me how this incident changed what would normally be seen as a family tragedy into an experience of peace, of resolution, of being assured that the Lord was aware and was with them in their hour of loss. They knew there was some kind of divine purpose in this seemingly random accident.

At the funeral service, the family displayed on the guest-book table a color photograph of the dove, perched on the jagged branch end, physical evidence to them of the Lord's care and love and assurance that the spirit of their departed husband, father, and grandfather was indeed alive and numbered among those in the paradise of God. In the services, one family member reported seeing the dove flying over the chapel as they had entered, and another talked about how the dove had revisited the family at their home more than once in the days between the accident and the funeral.

Such striking and clear examples of spiritual help when tragedy strikes do not happen with every loss of a loved one, or at other times when we experience undeserved pain from various causes during our stay here on earth. But I am convinced the Lord is aware of our pain and stands ready to bless and comfort us through whispered peace and encouragement, if we but listen for his quiet knock and the still, small voice of reassurance.

In addition to his statement in the Beatitudes, "Blessed are they that mourn: for they shall be comforted" (Matthew 5:4), the Lord also promised during his mortal ministry, "I will not leave you comfortless: I will come to you" (John 14:18). I believe that his divine comfort is available to us in all our infirmities and pain, especially those that seem visited upon us by seemingly random or capricious circumstances. When we fail to listen or are not aware of this important role of the Holy Spirit in the lives of active and committed Latter-day Saints, we lose one of the most important ways the Lord has provided to alleviate the pain that comes to us, and we instead choose misery and suffering.

A striking example of failure to heed the Spirit through prolonged or extraordinary grieving is recorded in the history of Marriner W. Merrill, an apostle and member of the Quorum of the Twelve in pioneer times. He was one of the earliest pioneers in Cache Valley, and was for many years president of the Logan Temple. Involved with many Church duties, Elder Merrill relied on his oldest son and namesake for managing the many economic interests he and his family were involved in.

In the prime of life, this son suddenly died. For many weeks Elder Merrill grieved for his son and had great difficulty accepting his passing. One day as he was traveling by horse and carriage from Logan back to his home in Richmond, about ten miles to the north, the following incident occurred:

> He sat in his carriage so deeply lost in thought about his son that he was quite oblivious to things about him. He suddenly came into a state of awareness when his horse stopped in the road. As he looked up, his son stood in the road beside him. His son spoke to him and said, "Father, you are mourning my departure unduly. You are over concerned about my family (his son left a large family of small children) and their welfare. I have much work to do and your grieving gives me much concern. I am in a position to render effective service to my family. You should take comfort, for you know there is much work to be done here and it was necessary for me to be called. You know that the Lord doeth all things well." So saying, the son departed.

After this experience, Elder Merrill was comforted, for he realized that the death of his son was in keeping with God's will. (Bryant S. Hinckley, *The Faith of Our Pioneer Fathers* [Salt Lake City: Deseret Book, 1956], 182–83.)

I'm convinced that the comfort offered by the Lord is there to help us bear our burdens and pain, if we will but open our hearts and spiritual senses and let him provide that divine comfort. Pain is inevitable in this earthly journey, but this is where we make the choice either to choose misery or to endure the pain well through heeding and accepting the comforting hand of our Lord and Savior, Jesus Christ.

As I contemplate the pain that all of us are called upon to endure in the mortal experience, I believe the only way we will ultimately be able to endure that pain well is to be in a spiritual condition that will allow us to receive the divine help that is available to us. We will all be visited by pain in our lives, but the Lord hasn't left us without the ability to endure it. As promised to Joseph Smith in the Liberty Jail and recorded in Doctrine and Covenants 121:8, "If thou endure it well, God shall exalt thee on high."

As I have pondered this scripture, I feel that all of us have been given the innate ability to endure our afflictions "well," and the Lord will help us to do so. I think it is not inappropriate to suppose that the angel who ministered to our Savior during his supreme agony in the garden of Gethsemane might have comforted and encouraged Jesus with words similar to those spoken more than 1,800 years later to one of his servants, the Prophet Joseph.

From my own experience, I know that sometimes "enduring" is all we can do with the pain and afflictions that come to us either unbidden or of our own doing. But that enduring can be borne more easily when we keep faith and hope "smiling brightly before us." (*Hymns* [Salt Lake City: The Church of Jesus Christ of Latter-day Saints, 1985], no. 19.) If we are willing to order our lives in such as way as to be spiritually sensitive enough to recognize the comforting promptings of the Spirit when they come, we will be given the power to "endure it well" rather than dwell in a state of misery.

CHAPTER 6

AVOID THE PAIN THAT COMES FROM SELF-DECEPTION

As the happiness or real good of men consists in right action, and right action cannot be produced without right opinion, it behooves, above all things in this world, to take care that our own opinion of things be according to the nature of things.

—Benjamin Franklin

Perhaps no emotional or spiritual pain is more excruciating than that we inflict upon ourselves. Most often we do this when we deceive ourselves about what is truly happening in a situation, denying the reality of what we are doing and its eventual effects and results.

My own experience with allowing myself to be, in Mother Eve's words, "beguiled" by the adversary taught me some painful but redemptive lessons about how I must seek to identify and live by the correct and true principles the Lord has provided. One of the most important of these lessons is the *absolute* necessity of making sure that what we believe to be true is aligned as closely with reality as possible, not just in this world but also in the eternal realms. If we are not living in sync with what is really true in the eternal sense, we can deceive ourselves about some very important matters and find ourselves in big trouble.

For most of my adult life I have been intrigued with why we do some of the things we do, and how we can change our behavior for the better. I read a lot about motivation and behavior change, and when I served as a mission president in California in the late 1970s, I tried to motivate and inspire our missionaries to be the best representatives of the Lord they could be. After being released from my service as president in 1981, I felt confident enough about my ability as a motivational speaker to go into business giving motivational seminars.

I later joined forces with others having similar interests, and with several of them eventually formed Franklin Quest, an organization that would later merge with Covey Leadership to form today's Franklin Covey Company. In 1984, at the beginning of what eventually became a very large venture, our focus was on time management and helping people make more effective and meaningful use of their time. In addition to training people in the use of our Franklin Day Planner, we also taught them about the importance of identifying and living by their inner governing values—the things that really mattered most to them in their lives.

In early 1985, two individuals, Jerry Pulsipher and Kurt Hanks, approached our organization with some ideas they had been developing. One of these was the metaphor of the Belief Window. This invisible window, they said, filters everything we see and experience, and our perceptions—so filtered— affect the decisions we make, the actions we take, and ultimately the results we get. Their basic premise was that since our behavior is significantly influenced by what we believe to be true about ourselves and the world, behavior change could take place only when an "incorrect" belief on a person's window was replaced by a better belief, one more in line with reality.

I was intrigued by this idea, and we eventually hired Jerry and Kurt to integrate some of their thinking with our ideas about helping people live in accordance with their governing values. Kurt and Jerry, and our president at the time, Bob Bennett (now serving as a United States senator), collaborated to write a book that explored the idea of the Belief Window and a process based on it that was later called the Reality Model. My full conversion to the power and potential of the Belief Window concept came in one of the most electrifying teaching situations I have ever experienced.

I was part of a cooperative anti-drug effort that also involved the U.S. Attorney's Office and the Utah Jazz basketball team in a series of assemblies at high schools all over Utah. One of the last of these assemblies took place in a high school in a southern Utah community. Because of the travel distance and other factors, the Jazz player who usually accompanied us couldn't go, and I found myself sitting with an assistant U.S. attorney in front of a hostile audience of students who had been preselected by the principal because they were known to have drug or alcohol problems.

With audience behavior indicating that these students were obviously not at all interested in hearing from the "suits" up front, I realized it would do no good to attempt the usual "don't do drugs" pep-talk I had been giving to student body assemblies elsewhere. As I stood to talk, I was strongly impressed to talk to these kids about the fact that they all have Belief Windows, and that what they were doing in their lives was determined to a significant degree by the beliefs they had placed on those windows. I also hauled several very reluctant kids up to the stage to serve as Belief Windows and other parts of the Reality Model. As I tried to help them understand the concepts, there were jeers and catcalls from the group, but I was determined to teach these concepts to these kids if it was the last thing I did.

After just one class period that seemed like an eternity, they were getting it and starting to apply the concepts to their own lives. When lunchtime came, the group wanted more and asked to come back after lunch for another period. Imagine my surprise and delight when I realized that these young men and women—probably the toughest, meanest group I've ever had to teach—were really starting to understand that beliefs like "drugs and alcohol are fun" would not really meet their needs over time.

At the end of the session, the kid who had been the ringleader of the group came up to me and said, "Let me tell you something. I've been in drug and alcohol therapy for ten years. I've been in jail four times. I've had every shrink in this state try to figure me out. But this is the first time anything made any sense to me." I reminded him that he was in charge of what stayed on or was taken off his Belief Window, and I gave him a challenge: "Are you man enough to take that window off, put it on the table, and find out if those beliefs are correct?" He straightened his shoulders and said, "Yeah, I am."

I later found out that this young man had accepted and lived up to that challenge. The drug and alcohol specialist from the school district where I had taught told me this young man had been mature enough to replace some of his destructive beliefs with ones that were serving him much better. He had graduated from high school and gone on to college. He also said that several others in the group had cleaned up their act and made some major changes in their lives.

After that experience I taught the Belief Window idea in more and more of my keynote speeches and presentations. In the past decade I have spoken to audiences all over the world, preaching the gospel of making sure that what we believe to be true—about ourselves, about other people, about the world, and about our place in it—really is in line with reality. In recent years I have felt such passion about these concepts that I, along with several others, formed The Galileo Initiative, a separate company specifically dedicated to teaching people and organizations to see through their Belief Windows more clearly, to change beliefs that do not meet the reality standard, and thus to make better decisions and change inappropriate or destructive behavior. In short, to see clearly and success-fully negotiate the bumpy road of mortality, the things we believe to be true must, in reality, *be* true.

And what is truth and reality? A common belief abroad in the world today is that our individual perceptions are, in fact, our reality. That's true, to a point, but I would suggest that it would be more accurate to say that our perceptions are our *perceived* reality. And I would also suggest that in spite of the billions of different "realities" that all who are now living might simultaneously have, there is still the reality that consti-tutes what's really out there. I have always liked the scriptural and inspired definition of truth and reality as taught by Jacob, Nephi's younger brother: "The Spirit speaketh the truth and lieth not. Wherefore, it speaketh of things as they really are, and of things as they really will be; wherefore, these things are manifested unto us plainly, for the salvation of our souls." (Jacob 4:13.)

Note that Jacob is talking about the necessity of understanding things as they *really* are and will be, not as we wish they were, or hope they will be. Be aware that the Spirit manifests "these things . . . unto us plainly, for the salvation of our souls." Truth and reality are there plainly, especially when revealed or confirmed to us by the Holy Ghost, giving us the sure standard against which all things can be measured. I'll have more to say about that in a later chapter, but for now I plead with you, as one who knows from painful experience, to take heed that you do not deceive yourself into believing that right is wrong and wrong is right or that wrong can somehow be justified. Convincing you to believe just that is one of the adversary's most subtle weapons, especially for those of us who have testimonies, who have received the witness of the Spirit in our lives, who consider ourselves to be active and devoted followers of Jesus Christ. After all, Satan doesn't usually have much success overtly tempting active Latter-day Saints to kill, or steal, or commit other obvious violations of the basic commandments. But he does make inroads into our souls by tempting us with subtly crafted counterfeits of things that appear to be good or at least not all that bad. And, over time, he can even lead us to believe that right is wrong and wrong is right. Believe me, I know.

Even when we know that something is clearly wrong, the adversary works to deceive us into justifying what we are doing. Active Latter-day Saints are usually pretty deeply ingrained with a sense of what is right and wrong, but we are less likely to be taught about the gray area in between where we often find self-justification for our transgressions.

From my own experience I am convinced that sin and transgression are in almost every circumstance a result of some degree of self-deception. We put on our Belief Windows ideas like "My parents didn't love me enough, so I feel the need to . . ." or "God will understand (or forgive me later)," or "This is no big deal" (when it really is), or more dangerously, "I'm a special case and it's okay for me to do this even when the scriptures say otherwise." Acting through a blur of incorrect beliefs on our windows, we justify our transgressions and would probably be horrified to realize that we are accepting the erroneous Belief Window Nephi spoke of in referring to those of our day: "There shall also be many which shall say: Eat, drink, and be merry; nevertheless, fear God—he will justify in committing a little sin. . . . There is no harm in this; and do all these things, for tomorrow we die; and if it so be that we are guilty, God will beat us with a few stripes, and at last we shall be saved in the kingdom of God." (2 Nephi 28:8.)

With that on your Belief Window, you will find yourself deceived, and, as Nephi graphically describes later in that same chapter, "thus the devil cheateth [your] souls, and leadeth [you] away carefully down to hell. . . . And thus he whispereth in [your] ears, until he grasps [you] with his awful chains, from whence there is no deliverance." (2 Nephi 28:21, 22.)

I don't mention all of this to make myself look good or possessed of superior wisdom. I firmly believe that these concepts are true, that we do need to take care that we are not deceived, that what we believe to be true in mortality is, in fact, true—reflecting "things as they really are."

In the presentations I make about the Belief Window, I teach people that if the results of their behavior are not meeting their needs over time, the problem is usually a belief on their windows. Conversely, behavior that is meeting needs over time is a good indication that a belief or beliefs are, in fact, in line with "things as they really are." So you can imagine my own painful "aha" that October Sunday in 1998 when I realized that my own behavior was *not* going to meet my needs over time.

As I watched general conference on television that day, Elder Jeffrey R. Holland's words about repentance cut through my soul like a hot sword. I had been living a lie for some time, and I knew it. I had rationalized and justified my behavior for too long, and now I clearly saw things as they really were. I saw that my eternal life, my eternal relationship with my wife and family, all that was precious and dear to me was teetering on the edge, and I knew that I was clearly in danger of having Satan grasp me "in his awful chains, from which there is no deliverance."

I have never felt greater spiritual pain. Not only had I violated an important commandment of our Heavenly Father, but my pain was doubly acute because I realized I had been guilty of doing exactly what I had been teaching people to avoid in almost all of my speeches and presentations for the previous decade. I berated myself terribly. How could I have so deceived myself? What was I thinking? What did I have on my Belief Window to have produced this behavior and these devastating results?

Among the most important lessons I have learned since that October day, patiently taught and reinforced by the Spirit, are these:

1. We are capable of rationalizing and justifying in our minds almost any kind of behavior. Especially if we have the belief on our windows that we are a "special case," that the rules

and commandments don't apply to us in the same way they do to other people, we stand in danger of justifying to ourselves almost any transgression. That's one belief to work hard to keep off your window. Remember and imprint on your soul this truth: *The Lord is no respecter of persons but loves all equally.* Likewise, the commandments apply equally to all, especially to those of us who know them and have received a testimony from the Holy Ghost of their divine origin and importance to our salvation.

2. The pain that comes from the realization that we have deceived ourselves in our transgression is acute, made so by the inner realization that we have betrayed ourselves and in the process have betrayed the Savior by treating his atoning sacrifice for us as if it were a thing of naught. My recognition of that reality pained me as much as anything else.

3. Our Father in Heaven's love for us never falters, even when it must seem to him that we have almost completely lost our way in the mists of darkness. A loving parent, he waits patiently for us to see the light, to realize what we have done or are doing, and to turn our faces once again to that light. He waits with open arms to wipe away the tears, to take away the pain, to welcome us back on the road toward home, and ultimately to welcome us again to our heavenly home.

4. Though our "sins be as scarlet" (Isaiah 1:18), the process of repentance and course correction given us by the Lord really works. Like so many things in the gospel, this sacred process is simple but profound, and it provides the way for us to overcome our self-deception and imperfections and, ultimately, to return to our Father with honor.

So how do we avoid self-deception, and how do we overcome it if we are already in its grip? The answer lies in regularly taking off your Belief Window and examining what you have placed upon it. First of all, let me talk a little more about Belief Windows and how they relate to who we are as children of God, and how they influence our behavior and results during our journey back to our Heavenly Father.

MEET YOUR BELIEF WINDOW

In scientific, psychological terms, the Belief Window is part of that area of the mind that represents consciousness, our sense of self. In gospel terms, it would be part of the soul, part of the spiritual DNA we talked about in chapter 4—the heart of the eternal, spiritual part of our being that came with us from our heavenly home, that identifies us as unique children of our Father in Heaven. In both psychological and gospel terms, the Belief Window is the repository of all our mortal experiences and what we have learned—correctly or incorrectly—from those experiences. However you view the person that is uniquely you, looking out at the world and trying to make sense of it, remember that everything you see is filtered through your Belief Window. Therefore, filtered through it are all the bits of processed sensory information you have placed on it through the years.

Our incomplete vision and unquestioning acceptance of what is on our windows is the cause of most of our problems in life, especially when our windows contain some deeply rooted beliefs that just don't reflect "things as they really are." Because we think we're sensing things correctly, we make decisions and act on those assumptions, sometimes ending up with results we don't like or that are actually harmful to us. For example, your prior experiences and social feedback may have caused you to believe all kinds of things—that you are smart, stupid, beautiful, ugly, competent, incompetent, creative, or dull—regardless of whether any of those beliefs are, in fact, true. And those and other beliefs on your window— whether true or untrue—exert the same powerful influence on your actions and behavior.

While the results of holding those beliefs can be considered as good or bad, it is important to understand that your Belief Window itself is neither "good" nor "bad." It is just *there*—the receptacle of all these perceptions that you believe are correct. Typically, the older you are, the more beliefs you have.

What Is Written on Your Belief Window?

So what's on your Belief Window? What have you placed on it that you *believe to be true* about the patterns you see in the world, yourself, and other people? These perceptions might be as simple and obvious as "Objects will fall to the ground when dropped from the top of a building" or "Antibiotics kill bacteria that cause infections." These two examples illustrate things we accept as true, based on scientific evidence and testing and proven through experience to be "correct" beliefs or principles—reflecting reality, or things as they *really* are.

This doesn't mean that incorrect perceptions on our Belief Windows doom us to poor decisions and failure. As we move through life and gain more experience, we modify and change many of the incorrect principles we previously held. A bad experience with a dog as a child may have given us the perception that all dogs are vicious and mean. Later experiences may help us realize that dogs can also be good friends and companions, even though some can be vicious. Looking at our gawky adolescent self in the mirror may give us the belief that we are the ugliest person on earth and affect our actions for a while, but as we grow into that nose or assume more adult looks, our "improving" image in the mirror and positive feedback from others can change what we had previously considered to be a devastating truth.

Some beliefs on our windows arise from the culture in which we live, not necessarily from our own experience. Because we grow up in a culture, we naturally tend to think that our experiences and perceptions are essentially similar to those of other people. We don't question many elements in our family or community dynamic or other early experiences, because we have no evidence that they may be based on faulty or incorrect ideas. We just assume that's the way things are. *Mommy and Daddy are always fighting. Times when I'm happy are few and far between. I'm hungry a lot.* To a child who doesn't know anything else, such perceptions can come to erroneously represent things as they really are for everyone else, too. If some of the worst of these perceptions end up causing us pain well into our lives, we could easily think that such results are natural and part of living, when in reality they are not representative. It's easy to see how easily things like child abuse in one generation can lead to child abuse in succeeding generations.

Such culturally based beliefs are often difficult to recognize and change, but with time and experience—and especially with the divine influence of the Holy Spirit in leading us "into all truth" (see John 16:13)—we can learn correct principles to replace faulty old ones. That's why the conversion experience is so powerful and life-changing. The Holy Ghost reveals to us "things as they really are," and our erroneous beliefs and resulting behavior can change almost instantaneously. With the repentance that often accompanies the conversion process, combined with a clearer view of reality brought by the Spirit, Belief Windows change, hope emerges, faith increases, and pain from past transgressions is taken away.

Remember also that just because a belief is widely held to be true does not make it so. The belief that the sun revolves around the earth, once widely held by many people, has in recent centuries been proven by scientific observation to be incorrect, not congruent with reality. Today, a large number of people feel that God is a myth, a construct of collective imagination, and that only unsophisticated people could believe in such a being. However widely held that view may be, it does not alter the truth as revealed by the Holy Spirit that God is indeed real, and that his reality can be sensed and known only through the help of the Spirit.

The sad account of Korihor is perhaps the best scriptural example of one who found himself in great spiritual danger because of self-deception. Not only did he have some erroneous beliefs on his window, but he also sought to convince others that his beliefs were correct. His argument sounds like those we hear today from atheists and agnostics. Look at what he revealed about the contents of his own Belief Window. "O ye that are bound down under a foolish and a vain hope, why do ye yoke yourselves with such foolish things? Why do ye look for a Christ? For no man can know of anything which is to come. Behold, these things . . . are foolish traditions of your fathers. How do ye know of their surety? Behold, ye cannot know of things which ye do not see; therefore ye cannot know that there shall be a Christ." (Alma 30:13–15.)

The record continues, "And thus did he preach unto them, leading away the hearts of many, causing them to lift up their heads in their wickedness." (Alma 30:18.) Alma's debate with Korihor teaches some powerful lessons about beliefs and reality. He not only made the scriptural case for a Heavenly Father and Christ but he also asked Korihor if he would still "deny against all these witnesses" as given by the prophets down through the ages. Korihor then asked for a sign and was struck dumb. Confronted with the evidence of "things as they really are," Korihor realized too late that the devil had deceived him. He had knowingly taught things that were untrue, and he admitted, "I taught them because they were pleasing unto the carnal mind . . . insomuch that I verily believed that they were true; and for this cause I withstood the truth, even until I have brought this great curse upon me" (Alma 30:18–53.)

So some of the principles we have placed on our Belief Windows may be strongly backed by scientific evidence and some from observing consistent patterns over time, true beliefs that are widely held in our communities or our culture at large. Others have come to us through the ministrations of the Holy Spirit, and we know them to be good and true and productive of good results in our lives. Wherever our own set of beliefs about ourselves and the world have come from, and regardless of whether they reflect reality or fantasy, it's important to remember this important fact: Regardless of whether the beliefs on our Belief Windows are true or not, we *believe* them all to be true. And because we believe them all to be true, we will *act* as if they are true.

HOW TO MAINTAIN A CLEAN AND REALISTIC BELIEF WINDOW

So how do you use this new awareness of your Belief Window to avoid self-deception? May I suggest that you frequently follow this simple process to check your Belief Window:

1. *Realize that you have a Belief Window* and that each day you place beliefs on it that are your perceptions of what you believe to be true about you, the world, and your place in it. The perceptions placed upon your Belief Window influence everything you do.

2. *Look at the results you are getting in life.* Will they meet your fundamental needs *over time* for security, love, and meaning? Do these results bring you happiness? Do you feel that you are making progress along the road to eternal life? Such results are the kind you want. If you are getting them, you must be doing some things right. On the other hand, are you getting some results that bother you or make you uneasy? Do they seem out of harmony with the gospel? Do they produce pain in your life? Try to understand what you are feeling about both the positive and negative results you are getting.

3. *Ask yourself what behaviors in your life are producing those results.* Be as specific as you can about anything in your behavior that may be contributing to the results. Is a feeling that you are less in tune with the Spirit a result of getting out of the habit of daily prayer? Could failure in an important relationship have anything to do with the fact that you have not done anything to nourish it in recent months? If you look backward from the results you are getting in a particular situation, you'll probably be able to identify behaviors or actions on your part that have contributed to those results.

4. *Ask yourself what beliefs might be on your Belief Window that would contribute to those behaviors and results.* Identifying these beliefs may not be easy, but with reflection and honestly seeking the Lord's help, such insights can be obtained. Just

realizing that what you believe to be true can and does affect your behavior and its results is often enough to help you take off your Belief Window and see what's there. Keep in mind that more than one belief may be contributing to your behavior.

5. *Identify new beliefs that appear to more accurately reflect reality.* Sometimes the opposite of the incorrect belief provides an avenue to a more realistic belief. The belief that "I am a special case in God's eyes" seemed so arrogant when I realized that it was actually on my own window. Certainly the more appropriate belief, "All are alike in God's eyes," comes closer to reality than the distorted idea that had been part of my clouded window.

6. *Identify and implement behaviors that will reinforce your new beliefs.* For example, take the flawed but common belief that "if those who love me don't know what I'm doing, it's doesn't harm anyone but me." An obviously better belief might be, "Trust is the heart of any good relationship, and especially my relationship with those I love." Using that belief, it's easy to see a number of behaviors you could implement that would help build trust in you and show those you love that you trust them.

Always keep in mind that we can perform tests—either actively or through observation—to see if our beliefs are true, false, or just matters of opinion. The method scientists use can be helpful in your efforts to examine and test the beliefs on your window. Scientific inquiry looks at the patterns in the natural world and examines beliefs (scientists call them hypotheses or theories) about how things work in the physical world. Through testing those hypotheses and theories, they arrive at conclusions as to whether they are true, false, or—as is often the case—somewhere in between or incomplete. Through their efforts the world has been able to replace many incorrect beliefs with correct (or at least *more* correct) ones.

However, believing Latter-day Saints have additional means for ascertaining truth that go beyond what can be observed through the senses and evaluated on the basis of logic alone. We have the witness of the Holy Ghost, testifying that some principles are indeed correct. Whether by scientific testing or the assurances of the Spirit, it is possible to identify, as more or less correct, principles related to the world and mortality, as well as the many eternal truths that come from the scriptures or through direct communication from the Lord.

Our effort to examine the validity of our own personal beliefs is complicated by the fact that we put them on our Belief Windows and consider them as absolutely correct without knowing for certain whether they truly describe reality or are just misconceptions on our part. This lack of testing can cause trouble for us because—regardless of how sound our beliefs are—we conduct our lives as if everything written on our Belief Windows is true.

RESULTS OFTEN TAKE TIME TO MEASURE

I've already suggested that if the *results* of your behavior meet your needs, you probably have a correct belief. Conversely, if the results do not meet your needs, you can be fairly sure the belief in question is incorrect.

Let's put this to the test by giving you a personal example. Those who know me well may also know that I have had a problem with pushing beyond the speed limit when I drive, especially when I'm late for an appointment. In examining my own behavior in this respect, I think I have probably been acting on the belief (one that many others on the road seem to share) that "a competent driver like me can safely drive above the speed limit." And I have indeed driven that fast at times; a few years ago I seemed to have an especially close relationship with the Utah Highway Patrol.

Well, I'm still alive, so does this mean my beliefs about speed limits and my driving abilities are correct? Not necessarily. You see, *results often take time to measure.* If we touch something hot, we will know the results almost immediately. But the results of many other actions may take years to become evident.

But what if I have followed that belief my whole life and have never had an accident, or never even gotten a ticket? Is it a correct belief? Again, not necessarily. Sometimes, when we're operating on an incorrect assumption, we manage to beat the odds. Sometimes we're lucky. For this reason, it's often wise to perform two tests on some of our beliefs—one through our own experiences and one through the experiences of others. In this particular case, we could look at data regarding fast drivers—perhaps statistics about the average speed of drivers involved in traffic accidents, or drivers who ended up as traffic fatalities. Perhaps statistics about the frequency of accidents for both speeders and non-speeders would be relevant. Or maybe we could consider the potential impact of driving 85 miles an hour on such things as driving records and insurance premiums. Sometimes common sense or potential bad results may be enough, as it has been in my case, to cause me to look for better beliefs. "Safety is more important than punctuality" is probably a more reasonable alternative.

Buying the incorrect principle that "the speed laws don't apply to me" also suggests other beliefs at work. One of these may be "it's okay to leave late for appointments." "Being late for appointments is bad for business" might be another. Perhaps changing one of these other beliefs will make the speeding belief irrelevant. "Arriving late for an appointment isn't the end of the world" would be an example. Or perhaps "Leaving early for appointments is a must." Another might be "Not breaking the law is important to me." Any of these Belief Window assumptions would eliminate the perceived need to rationalize speeding, and this has been an interesting and sometimes painful experience for me as I've examined my own Belief Window in this regard.

GROWTH IS THE PROCESS OF UPDATING YOUR BELIEF WINDOW

Personal growth is, in part, the process of challenging and updating what is on your Belief Window. The first step is accepting the possibility that some of the things on your window are wrong, and this may be powerfully brought home through painful experiences. But the willingness to recognize the need to question and change your Belief Window is a sign of maturity.

In the gospel context, we have the added assurance that the principles we learn from the scriptures and those taught by ancient and modern prophets are indeed correct principles, true beliefs, consistent with reality. These principles have been proven to be correct through thousands of years, and many of them form the basis for the laws that are the underpinnings of our judicial system. We can trust them and place them on our

Belief Windows with the confidence that they will serve us well in meeting our needs over time.

Conversion to the gospel of Jesus Christ is a powerful example of replacing incorrect beliefs and principles with correct ones. In this situation, we are dealing with identifying and incorporating into our lives correct principles that are essential to our personal salvation. These include such important truths as "We are all sons and daughters of a loving God who wants us to become like him" and "Through obedience to the laws and ordinances of the gospel, all of us can be saved and live again with our Father in Heaven and his Beloved Son."

The miracle of conversion occurs when we realize that these are not principles that reason alone can show to be correct. When confirmed by the ministrations of the Holy Spirit, these principles then go on our Belief Windows to form a powerful foundation to everything else. Once we have received that sacred witness that these principles and others related to them are true, not only are our Belief Windows changed but also our lives—forever.

As we have already discussed, repentance also has much to do with the process of changing incorrect principles that we have placed on our Belief Windows. I have learned important lessons from the application of our Savior's loving atonement in my behalf, and I am deeply grateful that in my own travails, my firm assurance about the fundamental principles mentioned above were there as beacons to help guide me through the darkest period in my life.

In repenting of sin, we must first realize that we have made a serious mistake and have been operating from a basis of incorrect beliefs or flawed perceptions of correct principles. Several flawed beliefs I had placed on my own Belief Window got me into trouble, and for too long I clung to them in an attempt to justify or rationalize actions that I inwardly knew were wrong. They got me into trouble because I uncritically accepted them as true. I didn't ask myself if they would meet my needs over time, and then I acted in accordance with those totally incorrect perceptions. I bought into Satan's subtle message of self-gratification and self-deception.

Whatever you may need to repent of, you'll most likely find an incorrect or inappropriate belief on your Belief Window that has led to or allowed the behavior to take place. So in order to change your behavior, you must first change the incorrect belief or beliefs. Perhaps you will need to realize and fully come to believe the correct principle that, under the Lord's plan of salvation, *we are each responsible for our behavior.* Perhaps you will need to come, as I did, to a full realization of and belief in the true principle that *we are God's children, and that our Heavenly Father loves us and will help us through the process of repentance.* Once this correct principle has been firmly placed on your Belief Window, much of the battle will have been won, and you will be on the way to changing the inappropriate behavior. This is not to say that you will be full of light and good cheer from that point on as you try to change your behavior and make restitution, but you will have begun the essential process.

Full repentance involves more than just recognizing that we have transgressed, changing the incorrect beliefs that contributed to it, making appropriate restitution, and "going our way and sinning no more." (See D&C 6:35.) There is at least one other person we need to bring into the process—our Savior, Jesus Christ. The "godly sorrow" that needs to accompany repentance comes from our full realization of the true principle that the Savior took upon himself all of our sins; therefore, we are partly responsible for his pain and suffering. I have felt real agony for the pain and anguish he suffered in that garden and on the cross in my behalf. Completing the process of repentance involves going with Jesus Christ to the garden and the cross and sharing with him some of the sorrow he experienced for you. Only then will his peace come into your heart, the release that comes from the Spirit, who testifies that the Lord has forgiven you, and you will once again feel enveloped by his love.

Serious transgression also requires visiting with your bishop, who can officiate and minister in behalf of the Church and will be an earthly source of understanding and support as you move through the process of changing your behavior and those incorrect beliefs on your window. A special part of the mantle bishops receive in their callings as judges in Israel is the ability to guide you with love and inspiration through what can be the most difficult time in your life. In the end, I testify again that it is worth it.

At this point, let's review some of what we've talked about in this chapter.

- Understanding the fact that much of our pain comes from our own self-deception establishes a foundation for making positive changes that will help alleviate the pain.
- Knowing that you have a Belief Window and that the beliefs you have placed on it may or may not be true or complete—that is, in line with reality—is a powerful tool in your journey to learn and live by the correct principles and laws the Lord has given us.
- What's written on your invisible Belief Window can be a

hindrance and a source of pain if you unquestioningly
accept everything on it as true.

- If, on the other hand, you are aware that some of the
beliefs written on your window are questionable and
need to be replaced with more correct beliefs, it can be
a powerful tool that can help you grow and change.

Sadly, in this imperfect mortal stage of our eternal existence, we can never hope to have perfectly clear Belief Windows
filled only with beliefs that reflect things as they really are.
Only one person, the Son of God, has gone through the mortal experience with a Belief Window that was totally clear and
filled with correct beliefs. But if we in our imperfection can be
aware that we each have a Belief Window, we can take it off
every so often, examine some of the things written on it, and
consciously look for more correct principles with which to
replace those that do not seem to reflect things as they really
are. To me, this is what eternal progression is all about.

And is not the purpose of our pain to help us make these
course corrections? To signal that it is time to check our Belief
Windows? To make adjustments? To grow because of those
adjustments? When we make this introspective process a firm
part of our lives, we will be far better equipped to avoid self-
deception and self-justification in both the temporal and spiritual aspects of our mortal experience.

I started out this chapter with a quotation from Benjamin
Franklin about how important it is for us that "our own opinion
of things [our beliefs] be according to the nature of things." I
close with another from this wise Founding Father: "Experience
keeps a dear [costly] school, but fools learn in no other."

I testify of the truth of both of those statements.

CHAPTER 7

TAKE THE HOLY SPIRIT AS YOUR GUIDE

When he, the Spirit of truth, is come, he will guide you into all truth.

—John 16:13

They that are wise and have received the truth, and have taken the Holy Spirit for their guide, and have not been deceived—verily I say unto you, they shall not be hewn down and cast into the fire, but shall abide the day. And the earth shall be given unto them for an inheritance.

—Doctrine and Covenants 45:57–58

The gift of the Holy Ghost is one of those things that I must admit I took too much for granted throughout most of my life. For many who have lived long within the gospel fold, the almost constant presence of the Spirit is with us in such a way that it's almost like the warming rays of the sun on a pleasant day—it's there, but we are not always consciously aware of it. Only when the Spirit is taken away do we realize what a precious gift it really is. Believe me, when it is taken away through transgression and ecclesiastical action such as excommunication, the loss is palpable, and feelings of great despair ensue.

When that most precious of gifts was taken from me for a

season, I longed for the familiar presence. And I was doubly grateful when the Lord granted me those rare and fleeting moments when the Holy Ghost was allowed to touch my spirit, to give me encouragement, to help me realize that I was not totally lost.

Having had the experience of the Spirit's complete withdrawal, I plead with you to fully appreciate the precious presence of the Holy Spirit in your life. Sometimes we are too much concerned with the things of the world, or, as novelist Edith Wharton many years ago wisely put it, "Some folks get themselves into the thick of thin things." But be assured that the Spirit is patiently there, waiting for you to listen to his still, small voice, and waiting to tutor you in the ways of the Lord and bless you. And in those moments when we feel any degree of the pain that comes from estrangement from the Lord, the Spirit is still there, never completely giving up on us, gently prodding and reminding us of the way back to full fellowship and communion with our Father in Heaven.

Years ago my friend and colleague, Jerry Pulsipher, had an experience with the Spirit that I think almost all Latter-day Saints can relate to. When he shared this experience with me recently, it resonated with my experiences in dealing with my own far weightier transgressions. I share it with you, with his permission, in part because Jerry told me that in his service as a bishop he shared the experience with a number of people— it was his testimony to them that the Lord knows each of us personally; that through the Holy Spirit he will take us by the hand, give us answers to our prayers, and ease our pains; and that the Holy Spirit teaches and guides each of us in ways we might understand only if we are in tune.

Jerry has always been a pretty obedient fellow and hadn't

felt that he had been guilty of any "big ticket" sins (at least any that had not long since been repented of). Jerry has had a number of callings in the Church and has tried to be a worthy husband, father, and priesthood holder. But, like all of us, he's not perfect. There are things he's done that he wishes he hadn't. There have been times in his life when he felt spiritually indifferent and, as he told me, felt that his prayers "weren't going above the ceiling" of his room. He's told me that there have been (and still are) times when, like most of us, he has felt lost, alone, and in spiritual pain.

September 1994 was one of those times. Even though Jerry was serving on the stake high council at the time, he felt that he had not been particularly close to the Spirit for many months, and he wasn't sure what was wrong. Something just sort of ached inside, and he longed for the closer spiritual presence he had felt in the past.

At the end of August, Jerry had his annual temple recommend interview with his stake president. In the interview the president had asked him the usual questions, including one about whether there was anything in his life that needed to be resolved by proper church authority. Jerry thought about it and answered, truthfully, he felt, that there was nothing that hadn't been resolved properly. Then the discussion got sidetracked on some other issues related to Jerry's calling on the high council.

Jerry continues: "When the president returned to the formal questioning, I was surprised that he went back to the same question I had already answered. He asked it again, almost as if he had forgotten that we had discussed this. I again didn't feel that there was anything that I needed to repent of or that needed discussion, and again I answered in the negative. At the end of the interview, he said he felt that I was worthy to enter the temple, and he signed the recommend. His asking the same question twice seemed unusual, and I briefly wondered if there actually was something in my life that I needed to look at, but the thought then passed from my mind."

A few weeks later, two events occurred that triggered some real soul-searching on Jerry's part. The first came in his ward's sacrament meeting, during the sacrament hymn. The congregation sang "Reverently and Meekly Now," a powerful hymn that to Jerry has had special meaning because the words are spoken in the first person, as if the Savior himself were speaking to us about his sacrifice and atonement. On this occasion, as they sang the first and second verses, Jerry felt a nudge from the Spirit in his heart, and tears began to well up in his eyes:

> *Rev'rently and meekly now,*
> *Let thy head most humbly bow.*
> *Think of me, thou ransomed one;*
> *Think what I for thee have done.*
> *With my blood that dripped like rain,*
> *Sweat in agony of pain,*
> *With my body on the tree*
> *I have ransomed even thee.*
>
> *In this bread now blest for thee,*
> *Emblem of my body see;*
> *In this water or this wine,*
> *Emblem of my blood divine.*
> *Oh, remember what was done*
> *That the sinner might be won.*

On the cross of Calvary
I have suffered death for thee.
—*Hymns,* no. 185

"As I sang these familiar words," Jerry told me, "I seemed to have a special feeling about what Jesus had suffered for me personally, that my sins might be forgiven and not be held to my account. I was grateful for this spiritual insight, but at the time I did not relate it to what had happened in the temple recommend interview two weeks earlier."

The second event was, like the experience with the hymn, completely unexpected. It occurred later that day when Jerry attended the high priests group meeting at the ward where he was assigned as high council representative. The lesson that day was on repentance, and during the lesson the instructor showed a video produced for the Church Educational System that dealt with the idea of "godly sorrow," a true recognition that the Savior suffered personally for each of our specific sins and shortcomings, and that we should truly feel sorrow for any pain we may have caused him to suffer for us.

"I had heard about godly sorrow before," Jerry said, "but somehow as I sat in the meeting this idea seemed to be tremendously important. All of a sudden my mind (and spirit) made an instant connection between my feelings about this lesson, my feelings during the hymn, and my earlier experience with President Walker in the interview. These three experiences all seemed to be telling me that I had not fully understood the process of repentance, and that there were things I needed to do about that to be whole before the Lord."

At the end of the class Jerry walked out of the chapel, deep in thought. All of a sudden the interview, the sacrament hymn, and the priesthood lesson all came together. "I felt that the Holy Ghost seemed to be orchestrating these things to get my attention. At first I wondered if I should go to President Walker and talk to him. Yet I wasn't really sure what I needed to talk with him about, if anything."

Jerry started driving toward the stake center and then had the feeling that he should turn around and drive up a nearby canyon into the mountains instead. "As I drove, I started to get answers, and things became clear about what I needed to do," he related, becoming more emotional with the retelling. "At this point, I was feeling real anxiety. I knew that the Spirit seemed to be orchestrating this personal learning experience, but I wasn't sure why or where it was going."

He realized that it was not the interview with the stake president that was his problem—there was nothing in his many imperfections and failings and shortcomings that hadn't been handled in the past or was serious enough to warrant confession before a bishop or stake president now. As he ascended the mountain road, a major "aha" flashed into Jerry's mind. In his words, "I realized that I had not completed a vital step in fully accepting the Atonement and making it completely available in my life. I had failed to contemplate and truly feel godly sorrow about any of the pain I had personally caused the Savior to suffer. Yet I knew that the Lord had already suffered and paid the price for my sins and shortcomings and pain. He was waiting for me to take the final step and accept the invitation he extends to us all to come unto him."

These thoughts pressed themselves powerfully on Jerry's mind and heart, and he described his feelings as he continued his drive up the canyon: "I felt an overwhelming desire to stop and find a place where I could be alone to pray and express my feelings to the Lord. But where to do it? The canyon seemed to have picnickers and hikers at every parking area." Finally, as the road crossed the stream, he noticed a small picnic area just beyond the bridge that was completely empty. There were no cars and no sign of anyone hiking or using the area. I'll let him describe what happened next:

"I pulled into the parking area, got out of my car, and walked down the trail on the south side of the creek, looking for a place where I could be alone and out of view. As I walked, I felt the Spirit quietly descend upon me. Unlike many previous experiences with the Holy Ghost, the Spirit this time did not bring peace to my soul. Instead, I felt deep anguish and sorrow about what the Savior had gone through for me in atoning for my sins and shortcomings. In my heart, I felt like I was watching him kneeling in the garden of Gethsemane, shaking and wracked with anguish that he was undergoing for me personally.

"I came to a picnic table that was fairly secluded, and powerful feelings rose from deep within me as I contemplated the Savior's agony. I just sat and wept, the tears rolling down my cheeks."

Then came a transformation that Jerry said was like going from night to day. Suddenly what had started out as bitter tears of anguish were transformed into sweet tears of joy and gratitude. "I knew that my repentance for so many, many things had been completed and was accepted by the Lord. I felt a burden lift from my shoulders—a burden now I realized had been there for a long time. I'll never forget the sense of freedom, the feelings of love that I felt through the Spirit, and the love that I felt my own spirit send back heavenward."

Jerry told me that after this transformation, he sat in silence, the tears still coming, just drinking in the peace that he now felt—at one with the mountains, the stream, the trees, and the beauty of the sunlight filtering down through the fir trees. Finally, with a profound feeling that he was whole and clean before the Lord, he walked back to his car. With deep gratitude in his heart, he drove back down the canyon to attend the sacrament service of his assigned ward, arriving just as the sacrament was being prepared. It was his second experience with this sacred ordinance that day, but one that after his tutoring by the Spirit now had special meaning.

According to Jerry, the most meaningful moment in the service came in listening to the sacrament prayers. "In my mind I changed those words slightly and personalized them to express what I was feeling, almost as a silent prayer of my own: . . . *that I am willing to take upon me the name of thy Son, and always remember him*—and in my mind I silently added, *and the pain I caused him to suffer for my transgressions*—*that I may always have his Spirit to be with me.* I partook with deepest gratitude and a renewed determination to *keep his commandments which he has given me.*"

Jerry's sacred learning experience with the Spirit echoed some of my own as I worked through the pain of my recent much more serious transgressions, and I reflected again on my own experiences with gratitude and wonder at how intimately the Lord knows each of us, and at how much he wants to be able to communicate with us in our darkest hours, to lift the burdens, to heal the wounds and the hurt, to relieve the pain and suffering, if we will but let him.

The Role of the Holy Ghost in Alleviating Pain

There's a reason why the Savior so frequently referred to the Holy Ghost as the Comforter. In addition to his other roles in leading us into all truth, bringing all things to our remembrance, testifying that Jesus is the Christ, and helping us not to be deceived by Satan's counterfeits, the Holy Spirit is most of all a source of encouragement and comfort to our Father's children as they make their way along the rocky road of mortality.

The term *comforter* brings to mind many happy associations—snuggling in a warm blanket as a child after playing outside or being comforted in the arms of a loving parent. I think that Jesus' use of the word to describe the Holy Ghost extends those childhood feelings as a beautiful metaphor for the divine measure of love and comfort that can be given us by a Heavenly Parent.

Along my own four-year-plus journey back to full fellowship with the Saints, there were many dark moments when I longed to be enwrapped in a heavenly blanket, to feel the comforting arms of the divine presence. This was especially acute as the gift of the constant companionship of the Holy Ghost was formally taken from me through excommunication.

As I went through the initial stages of my repentance process, one of the major sources of anguish was the worry that no one would forgive me. I also felt that I could never really forgive myself for the stupid things I had done. Somewhere in my experience in the Church, the belief had gotten into my mind that to be ultimately forgiven for a transgression, you also had to forget it. Maybe this was because we are taught in the scriptures that, when repentance is real and complete, the Lord forgets. But forgetting is a tough thing for mortals to do, both on the part of the transgressor as well those who are aware of the transgression.

Being somewhat of a high-profile person in business and in the Church, I was pained by the public humiliation I went through, including extensive newspaper articles discussing my excommunication. Such matters are usually held as confidential, and I was certain as my situation became public knowledge that anyone who knew me would neither forgive me nor forget the fact that I was a sinner. I was sure that even if I made it back, I would never be asked to serve again in a meaningful way, and that there would always be a certain amount of whispering going on behind my back.

Just as I was in danger of letting these dark thoughts send me into depression and debilitating self-loathing, the Lord must have recognized that I needed the Holy Ghost back with me, even if it couldn't yet be restored as a permanent gift. Deep in the middle of one of many walk-the-floor nights, the gentle touch of the Spirit taught me a great lesson: *Forgiveness doesn't mean forgetting. It means remembering, but it also means that remembering doesn't matter anymore.* That realization took away much of the self-punishment I was putting myself through and helped me to proceed on a more even keel. It didn't matter any more. All that mattered was moving beyond the pain and embarrassment and the discomfort to the goal of regaining my eternal salvation and my eternal family.

There were other times when the Holy Spirit was granted to me to help me stay on course. Over the months, those moments were times of increasing reassurance that the Lord still loved me and that, with patience and determination, I could find my way back. And finally there was the moment when I knew that the Lord had really forgiven me. The days, weeks, and even months following my excommunication had been a dark time. Not having the Holy Ghost present with you from day to day is a scary prospect, I assure you. In the two years that followed my excommunication in November 1998, there were three marvelous occasions when the Spirit bore witness to me in a clear, precise, and recognizable way that the Lord had in fact forgiven me of my transgressions.

In each case, these wonderful, peaceful confirmations of the Spirit came as a result of serious and searching prayer. Also, in each case, the prayer was sparked and motivated by some massive feelings of despair in wondering whether or not I would ever get through this process.

These three experiences were and are very sacred moments in my life. Because of this I won't go into the details of what occurred, but I will assure you that when the Spirit spoke, it was very real, and the overwhelming sense of peace that came to me on those occasions was an amazing thing to experience. This was made doubly so because the regular, daily gift of the Holy Ghost had been taken from me when I was excommunicated, and it meant so much to know that the Spirit could still be there for me on an emergency basis to help me through the Lord's cleansing process. There is no question in my mind that the Holy Ghost exists, that one of his primary functions is to testify to us and speak in behalf of the Lord in our lives. I am very grateful for these special moments of clear communication that came from my Father in Heaven, assuring me of (1) his love for me and (2) his forgiveness for what I had done.

After the third experience, I was confident enough that the Lord had forgiven me that I made an appointment with my stake president and in that meeting declared my redemption, much as Alma did when he came out of his coma after his three-day experience with the Spirit following the encounter with the angel on the highway. It was the most liberating and wonderful experience to be able to stand before my file leaders in the priesthood and declare unequivocally that the Lord had in fact forgiven me.

The fact that it took me six hundred days and Alma only three is interesting; that clearly shows that Alma was a considerably greater human being than I am. But, as with Alma, I knew that my repentance was acceptable to the Lord and that the painful process was nearly over. From that time forward, I felt my faith in the Lord and in the process of repentance both solidifying and strengthening beyond anything I had felt for a long time. The Holy Ghost had truly returned as my comforter.

In addition to being a source of comfort, the Holy Ghost also has the important role of helping us keep from being deceived—either by our own misperceptions or through the clever counterfeits that Satan uses to sidetrack us. In the forty-fifth section of the Doctrine and Covenants, the Savior powerfully illustrates this important role of the Spirit by referring to his parable of the wise virgins: "At that day, when I shall come in my glory, shall the parable be fulfilled which I spake concerning the ten virgins. For they that are wise and have received the truth, and have taken the Holy Spirit for their guide, and have not been deceived—verily I say unto you, they shall not be hewn down and cast into the fire, but shall abide the day. And the earth shall be given unto them for an inheritance; and they shall multiply and wax strong, and their children shall grow up without sin unto salvation." (D&C 45:56–58.)

The warning against being deceived is perhaps the most oft-repeated message that the Lord has given us in the Doctrine and Covenants, our prime book of latter-day scripture. Those assurances in section 45 give us the key to avoiding such deception, and they plainly indicate the role of the Holy Spirit in being our guide, keeping us safe, and enabling us to "abide the day" and its accompanying pain and anguish.

LEARN HOW THE HOLY SPIRIT SPEAKS TO YOU

Because our relationship with the Holy Spirit is shaped by our unique personalities and our individual experiences and perceptions as we mature and come to realize its presence, it is a very personalized and individualized relationship. It also reflects our uniqueness as spirits endowed with special characteristics created by a loving Father in Heaven. The manifestations of the Spirit will vary between individuals, and how the Lord speaks to me through the Holy Spirit may be different in some respects from the way he will speak to you. Because the adversary is always seeking to confuse us or divert us from the ways of the Lord, it is vital for us to know for a surety the ways in which the Spirit speaks to us. Without that knowledge, we run the danger of being deceived by one of Satan's clever counterfeits, including those through which he can encourage our own self-deception.

So if one of the greatest challenges that we have in mortality is to learn to recognize the promptings of the Spirit when they come, how can we be sure that we are getting an answer from the Holy Ghost? I have long felt that the best, most powerful, and most accurate test that something is true and of God is the witness of peace. I believe there is only one emotion that the adversary cannot counterfeit or duplicate, and that is the emotion of peace. He may be able to counter-feit nearly the entire spectrum of human emotions, up to and including what we might even feel is a "burning in the bosom." Jesus himself declared in John 14:27, "Peace I leave with you, my peace I give unto you: *not as the world giveth, give I unto you.*" I have seen people get very excited about incorrect principles, false doctrine, or inappropriate behavior, claiming they have been told by the Spirit that this or that thing is true or appropriate. But I have also noticed on such occasions that they do not have a feeling of peace about the matter.

So to me, there is only one true witness that I believe will be part of any communication from our Father in Heaven, and that is the witness of peace. Reread the entire sixth section of the Doctrine and Covenants. Here the Lord is talking specifically to Oliver Cowdery and gives him some wonderful counsel. In verses 22 and 23, we are taught a marvelous principle: "If you desire a further witness, cast your mind upon the night that you cried unto me in your heart, that you might know concerning the truth of these things. *Did I not speak peace to your mind concerning the matter?* What greater wit-ness can you have than from God?"

What the Lord was reminding Oliver about was an appar-ent earlier inquiry when Oliver was having a struggle with his testimony of Joseph and the work. Oliver had gone to the Lord for help and had been blessed with a feeling of peace about the matter. In reminding Oliver of this, the Lord asks a potent question: "Is there any greater witness than from God?"

The close connection between the Holy Spirit and the kind of peace the Savior describes is amply attested in the scriptures. Paul especially focuses on this, promising to the Romans that "the God of hope [may] fill you with all joy and peace in believing, that ye may abound in hope, through the power of the Holy Ghost." (Romans 15:13.) To the Galatians he taught that "the fruit of the Spirit is love, joy, peace, long-suffering, gentleness, goodness." (Galatians 5:22.) Paul counseled the Philippians, "Be careful for nothing; but in every thing by prayer and supplication with thanksgiving let your requests be made known unto God. And the peace of God, which passeth all understanding, shall keep your hearts and minds through Christ Jesus." (Philippians 4:6–7.) And James, whose words about asking God for wisdom spoke through the Holy Spirit to Joseph Smith in 1820, talks about the nature of answers that we receive from our Father through the Spirit: "The wisdom that is from above is first pure, then peaceable, gentle, and easy to be intreated, full of mercy and good fruits." (James 3:17.)

To me, having a feeling of peace is vital when we are seeking a witness of the truth regarding anything—the reality of God and Jesus Christ, the truth of the gospel, the restoration of the priesthood, the correctness of a principle, and personal answers to questions. As we study these things out in our minds and then approach the Lord in humble prayer, with broken hearts and contrite spirits, we can do so with the assurance that we will be given a witness of the Spirit. It may come in different ways to each of us, but it will always include at some point the witness of peace. That peace will come as a benediction of truth to our minds, to our hearts, to every cell of our bodies, and it is a marvelous thing to experience.

Alma alludes to this in the fifth chapter of Alma, verse 14, where he asks us, as he did the people of Zarahemla, "Have ye spiritually been born of God? Have ye received his image in your countenances? Have ye experienced this mighty change in your hearts?" To be able to respond to those three questions in the affirmative—especially if you have gone through the process of spiritually being reborn of God—you will need to have had an experience with the peace of the Lord, the peace that "passeth all understanding." (Philippians 4:7.)

My counsel is to recall those moments when there was no question in your mind that you were in fact experiencing this kind of peace. What did that peace feel like? Where did you feel it? In your heart? In your mind? In your surroundings? How did you feel at that point? Remember those times when you have felt a special closeness in your communications with the Lord. Perhaps you were in the temple going through a session, taking a few moments in the Celestial Room to have a quiet word of prayer on your own, communicating directly with your Father in Heaven. Perhaps you were in a sacrament meeting, partaking of the emblems of the Lord's Supper. Or it may have been in a beautiful outdoor setting.

Wherever you were, you probably experienced some feelings that are beyond description. There may have been a calmness, a serenity, or an assurance of rightness, of truth. Perhaps there was an inner swelling of gratitude and love in your bosom and an upwelling that brought tears of joy to your eyes. There may have been a wonderful feeling of confidence in knowing that God was present and listening to your prayer and caring about who you are and what you are and where you're going. Those are all feelings of the Lord's peace that "passeth all understanding."

Or think back to moments alone or with your spouse

when you were praying together before going to bed, or in the morning before you started the day, or at a time of special need when you felt the Lord nearby. Was there a wonderful feeling of oneness with the Lord? If you were with your spouse, did you both feel the same recognition that the Spirit was there?

The Spirit can come to us individually as well as when we are with someone we love. There have been special times in my relationship with Gail when we have risen from our knees and looked at each other with tears in our eyes, and there was a spoken or unspoken mutual feeling that we both had felt something wonderful. Whether you have experienced those feelings alone or with someone else, those are the feelings you need to feel again, the feelings you want to watch for. So when you are seeking the answers to your prayers, seeking direction in your life, and seeking the truth of any principle you have identified, you want to be sure those feelings you know are from the Lord are there in the answers you get.

Now, the Lord isn't going to make all our decisions for us or make our pain go away just because we ask. When Oliver Cowdery sought the Spirit in attempting to translate from the gold plates, the Lord said, "Behold, you have not understood; you have supposed that I would give it unto you, when you took no thought save it was to ask me." (D&C 9:7.) He's not always going to tell us exactly which way we ought to go, but he will tell us whether the decisions we have made are right or wrong. He expects us to study it out in our minds, make the decision, and then come to him for the verifying power of the Spirit to let us know that we are in fact doing the right thing. Or that perhaps we're doing the wrong thing. Again, in verifying our answers, we are seeking those same wonderful feelings of peace that we have experienced in those sweet moments of our lives when we knew that peace was there.

Sometimes that peace comes when we are not seeking answers. We may feel it at times when we need the comforting assurance that the Lord is there, that he loves us, that he grieves with us, and that he will continue to be with us. At those times his "peace that passeth all understanding" can be the best pain reliever there is.

When you have such feelings, it might be a good idea to jot them down—*this was the date, this is where I was, this is what I was seeking, and these are the feelings that I had.* Then when you seek for further light and knowledge, when you seek relief or understanding of life's vicissitudes, you'll be looking for those same kinds of confirming feelings that you experienced before. And if they don't come, if other kinds of emotions come, know that they are probably not coming from your Father in Heaven. Although his communication may, when the need is there, be more dramatic—a vivid dream, an audible voice, or sudden knowledge springing into your mind—more generally the Spirit will speak to you in a consistent and familiar way. But however the Spirit speaks to you, it will usually at some point include the feelings of peace we've talked about.

Once you know what communication from the Lord feels like for you, then you can look for it as you search for truth in any aspect of your life—making a correct decision with a career; about whom you ought to marry; about whether or not you should go to school; about how to counsel a child, a spouse, or a friend.

Most important, seek the peace of the Spirit as you deal

with the weightier matters of life, especially the physical and spiritual pain we've been talking about in this book. As you seek for higher help in dealing with all of the pain and uncertainty that comes with mortality, look for the peace and comfort the Lord has promised us through the Holy Ghost. In the darkest of times, that reassuring presence, however dimly perceived amid the pain, will be the sure foundation that will carry you through to the dawning of a better day.

"PEACE BE UNTO THY SOUL"

No one knew better than Joseph Smith the role of the Holy Ghost in helping us deal with pain. By March 20, 1839, after a winter-long incarceration in the cramped, inhuman conditions of the misnamed Liberty Jail, Joseph had nearly reached the end of his rope. His followers had been dispossessed of their homes and belongings, scattered and driven eastward to the shores of the Mississippi River. The dream of building Zion lay shattered and broken in the now-deserted Missouri settlements. Deprived of knowledge about his family and friends, he must have wondered what the Lord was doing. The spiritual pain he felt must have been excruciating. Had he lost his way, lost the calling and mission the Lord had given him? Could the broken and scattered Church survive and rebuild itself? Would he ever again see his beloved Emma and their family? I'm sure that many "what if's" and doubts hammered at his soul.

Some of the agony he felt is so clearly evident in the eloquent and anguished opening words of his prayer to his Father in Heaven as recorded in section 121 of the Doctrine and Covenants: "O God, where art thou? And where is the pavilion that covereth thy hiding place? How long shall thy hand be stayed, and thine eye, yea thy pure eye, behold from the eternal heavens the wrongs of thy people and of thy servants, and thine ear be penetrated with their cries?" (D&C 121:1–2.)

And what were the first words of what I imagine was an equally anguished and concerned Father in Heaven? "My son, *peace* be unto thy soul." (D&C 121:7.) I can only imagine the comfort this communication through the Holy Spirit brought to Joseph at that time of pain and spiritual agony. But I know of a certainty and bear witness that the Father's blessing of peace to the Prophet Joseph was not reserved for him alone. Through the ministrations of the Holy Ghost, that same peace is available to all who "labour and are heavy laden." (Matthew 11:28.)

CHAPTER 8

"THAT THEY MIGHT NOT SUFFER"

Behold the outstretched hands of Christ,
Our God, who came to save.
Whose love and grace redeems our souls
And lifts us from the grave.
Though bruised and battered as we stray
His guiding hands caress.
He washes and anoints with oil.
Then in His arms we rest.

—John V. Pearson

Perhaps the most significant event in history happened at night in the garden of Gethsemane when the Savior began the atonement process. I have thought a great deal about that night in the garden, and particularly the past four or five years as I have discovered for myself the reality of the Atonement. What took place in those few hours has had a profound impact on me, and you, and all who have ever lived or will yet live.

A question has intrigued me as I consider that event: While the Savior was alone, in the rear part of the garden of Gethsemane, while his apostles were asleep at the gate, how and why did he bleed from every pore? That has caused me a

127

great deal of thought over the years. The Savior was alone in the garden. No one was there whipping him; he wasn't being beaten; he didn't yet have a crown of thorns on his head. The pictures of that event never seem to show agony sufficient to suggest the kind of physical and mental pain he must have been going through. Some of the paintings make him appear almost serene, in final communication with his Father before the harrowing events of the coming hours. What possibly could cause pain sufficient to produce spontaneous bleeding?

When we think about the Atonement, we tend to gloss over the intimate, almost quiet depictions of Christ in the garden and think more about the humiliation and excruciating pain he had to endure during the crucifixion. I have considered that maybe we do that because we don't want to consider what *we* did to him but would rather focus on what *they* did to him.

In the hours before he was placed on the cross, the Savior of the world had been mocked and spat upon, he had been cruelly whipped and beaten, and a crown of thorns had been pressed into his scalp. While all this was horrible enough, I can't conceive of the pain he suffered in being placed on the cross and having spikes driven not only through his hands but also his feet. All of that had to be incomprehensibly painful. Crucifixion was not an uncommon death in those days; many thousands of people died in this most cruel and inhuman way of taking life. But as horrible as that death must have been, we are taught in the scriptures that it was not the worst pain the Savior had to endure in the final hours of his mortal life.

In the nineteenth section of the Doctrine and Covenants, the Savior himself describes this pain he had to endure in Gethsemane, spoken as part of a solemn commandment and warning to each of us. Starting in verse 15 we read, "I command you to repent—repent, lest I smite you by the rod of my mouth, and by my wrath, and by my anger, and your sufferings be sore—how sore you know not, how exquisite you know not, yea, how hard to bear you know not."

We can sense a feeling of remembered anguish coming from our Savior in this verse as he recalls his experience, and I've always been fascinated by the fact that he used the word *exquisite* to describe the kind of pain he's talking about. Whenever I have personally used the word *exquisite,* it has been to describe a beautiful scene or painting. I have never thought of using the word to describe pain. Yet I found that one of the dictionary definitions of exquisite is "intense." And if you put the word *intense* in place of the word *exquisite* in verse 15 of section 19, it would read like this: "And your sufferings be sore—how sore you know not, how *intense* you know not, yea, how hard to bear you know not." The Savior is making a poignant point here: The pain that comes when we do not repent of sin is horrible.

How does he know how horrible that pain is? Let's go to verse 16: "I, God, have suffered these things for all, that they might not suffer if they would repent." Here he describes in his own words what he did in our behalf. He went through this excruciating experience so we wouldn't have to. None of us can fully understand how he did it, at least while we're in this life, but Jesus took upon himself the sins of the world, each and every sin of each and every human being who has been born or is still to come. Not only that, he also took upon himself the innumerable ways we fall short of the perfection he has told us we should seek, a perfection that only he among all who have lived was able to achieve in mortality. And when you personalize that and fully comprehend the fact that he has paid for our individual sins and shortcomings and that he has experienced the effects of them all, it makes it all even more incomprehensible and sobering, and yet even more wonderful. It is so incomprehensible I find myself frustrated trying to express in words what it really means.

Now let's go to verse 17: "But if they would not repent"—and here comes the warning—"they must suffer even as I." So the Savior is warning us that if we decide not to repent and avail ourselves of his atoning sacrifice, we'll have to go through what he who was *without* sin went through for our sake.

Then he describes something about this pain he endured for us, words that resonate in the depth of my soul every time I read the first few lines of verse 18: "Which suffering caused myself, even God, the greatest of all, to tremble because of pain, and to bleed at every pore, and to suffer both body and spirit."

This is the most powerful description in all scripture—given us by Jesus himself—of what happened in the garden of Gethsemane while his apostles slept near the gate. This is what happened to the Savior when he was alone, with no other person or thing there inflicting pain upon him. He makes it plain that the pain occurred not only physically but also in his soul, indescribable pain endured by our Elder Brother, the same one who volunteered in the great council in heaven to come to earth and perform this saving act that only a God could perform. And as mentally prepared as he must have been for this ordeal, this excruciating inner pain caused him to tremble, making all the more understandable the words he used to describe that experience to Joseph Smith: ". . . and would that I might not drink the bitter cup, and shrink."

We may never completely understand what caused the horrible pain that wracked the soul and body of the Savior in the garden of Gethsemane. It appears from both the scriptures and the words of the prophets that much of his suffering had to do with enduring the pain of experiencing—as the only one who ever lived a life without sin—and paying the price for the sins of all the rest of us who have and will come to earth.

As the English clergyman F. W. Farrar so beautifully describes in his classic book *The Life of Christ,* full comprehension of these events is beyond our mortal capacity:

> We may not intrude too closely into this scene. It is shrouded in a halo and a mystery into which no footstep may penetrate. We, as we contemplate it, are much like those disciples [dozing at the garden gate]—our senses are confused, our perceptions are not clear. We can but enter into their amazement and sore distress. Half waking, half oppressed with an irresistible weight of troubled slumber, they only felt that they were dim witnesses of an unutterable agony, far deeper than anything which they could fathom, as it far transcended all that, even in our purest moments, we can pretend to understand. The place seems haunted by presences of good and evil, struggling in mighty but silent contest for the eternal victory. They see Him, before whom the demons had fled in howling terror, lying on His face upon the ground. They hear that voice wailing in murmurs of broken agony, which had commanded the wind and the sea, and they had obeyed Him. The great drops of anguish which

fall from Him in the deathful struggle, look to them like heavy gouts of blood. (F. W. Farrar, *The Life of Christ* [Portland, Ore.: Fountain Publications, 1964], 624.)

In *The Mortal Messiah,* Elder Bruce R. McConkie quotes these words from Farrar and then adds authoritatively, referring to the great drops looking like heavy "gouts" of blood, "And so they were." ([Salt Lake City: Deseret Book, 1979] 4:127.)

Like Farrar, I am powerless to put into words what the Savior of the world was going through in those dark hours. Also like Farrar, I have tried to imagine what it would have been like to have been there that night. And I have pondered deeply what could have contributed to pain sufficient to cause the Savior to bleed from every pore. We know from the scriptures that much of the pain came from his assumption of our sins and shortcomings. But it also came because he was left to undergo at least part of this experience entirely on his own.

For all the years of his mortal life and ministry, the Savior's Father in Heaven was with him, perhaps even daily, sustaining and helping and inspiring his Son to do all the things he had to do in establishing the kingdom and bringing to pass the needed atonement for the Father's children. As suggested in D&C 76:107, the Savior had "overcome and . . . trodden the wine-press *alone.*" These words suggest that this was something he was required to do on his own, a time during which he could not receive help from his Father. Such a withdrawal of the Father's help must surely have contributed to his hesitancy about drinking "the bitter cup" and was the cause of his "shrinking" from the experience.

As Brigham Young taught, "The light, knowledge, power,

and glory with which [the Savior] was clothed were far above, or exceeded that of all others who had been upon the earth after the fall, consequently at the very moment, at the hour when the crisis came for him to offer up his life, the Father withdrew Himself, withdrew His Spirit, and cast a vail over him. That is what made him sweat blood. If he had had the power of God upon him, he would not have sweat blood; but all was withdrawn from him, and a veil was cast over him, and he then pled with the Father not to forsake him. 'No,' says the Father, 'you must have your trials, as well as others.'" (*Journal of Discourses*, 26 vols. [London: Latter-day Saints' Book Depot, 1854–1886], 3:206.)

Here was Jesus the Christ in the garden of Gethsemane, only a few hours away from completing the remainder of his mortal mission, the reason for his coming. I don't know what the conversation with his Father would have been, but it could have gone something like this: "My Beloved Son, I was with you in the beginning, when we laid the foundations of the earth. I've been with you all your mortal life, and I've been here for the past three years as you ministered to my children. But now, as you have known from the beginning, I can't help you through these hours. You've got to do this on your own. This is the part you have to do by yourself." And I can see that anguished Eternal Father withdrawing to the far corners of the universe.

I can also see how the Savior would then have experienced the depths of hell. What are the depths of hell if not the total absence of the Spirit of God? The overwhelming loneliness of such a separation would have been so wrenching to this Beloved Son—together with the burden of assuming all the sins, shortcomings, and imperfections of all who had lived or ever would live on earth—that it literally pulled the blood from his veins.

I also wouldn't be surprised if, as Lucifer made the case for why we should accept his plan in the premortal existence, part of his argument had to do with the almost impossible prospect of Jesus being able to endure and complete the atonement the Father's plan required. It could have been one of the reasons the adversary was able to persuade one out of three of all the spirits in heaven to his side in the conflict.

I can imagine a sales pitch that would have been something like, "Do you *really* think Jesus can do this by himself? There is no way he can do that. There isn't anyone in the universe who could do that alone and go through the pain such an atonement would require." And I can see one out of three—a third of the host of heaven—buying that pitch and going with Lucifer. But that would also mean that two-thirds, including you and me, individually decided, "You know, I think he *can* do this for us."

I wouldn't be surprised if all of us, prior to our birth, watched this event unfold in the garden, feeling for ourselves some of the agony he was enduring, pleading that he would be able to complete what needed to be done. If so, we were probably exercising the full measure of our faith and saying things like, "Jesus, we have trusted in your word, we trust you now, we love you, and we know you can do it." And in my mind's eye I can see us as an assemblage of spirits at a bittersweet event, our countenances reflecting joy and gratitude and anguish as we saw our own Elder Brother fulfill his promise and complete what he came to earth to do.

In Doctrine and Covenants 19:19, the Savior himself tells of that fulfillment: "Glory be to the Father, and I partook and finished my preparations unto the children of men." So he did it, he finished his preparations, he did what he promised us he would do. He kept his word. And all the children of God are blessed because he did so. The beautiful thing about it all is that Jesus Christ paid the price, he suffered and bled for us, and we owe it to him to see that those "preparations" for us were not made in vain.

Let's go to one more verse, 20, in section 19 of the Doctrine and Covenants. Joseph Smith received this revelation for Martin Harris, who had at some point experienced a loss of the Holy Ghost. After concluding his graphic account of his experience in the garden of Gethsemane, the Lord said to Martin Harris, "I command you again to repent, lest I humble you with my almighty power; and that you confess your sins, lest you suffer these punishments of which I have spoken, of which in the smallest, yea, even in the least degree you have tasted at the time I withdrew my Spirit."

We have talked about the process of repentance throughout much of this book: After recognizing that we have indeed sinned, we must be truly remorseful, we must turn away completely from the transgression, we must seek the Lord's forgiveness for what we have done, and we must commit ourselves fully to never doing it again. If we are guilty of major sin, as I was, we must also confess to our bishop and submit to any disciplinary action the Church may require for those transgressions.

There is one other important step in the process of repentance we seldom hear about: I believe that each of us, in his or her own way, must make our own journey in spirit back to that sacred garden—we must go alone to Gethsemane to be with the Savior there, to watch with him, and to witness through the Holy Spirit that portion of his agony he suffered for us personally.

Why is this important? Let me suggest a reason or two: When we sin, we withdraw ourselves from the Savior, and when we withdraw from the Lord we also experience a similar withdrawal of the Spirit from us. It's not as excruciating as the pain the Savior had to endure; it doesn't pull the blood from our veins. But our withdrawal certainly causes depression; it certainly causes us to go through all of the negative emotions that sin brings into one's life. As with many other matters discussed in this book, I speak from experience. Going to Gethsemane with the Savior allows us to better understand what he did there for each of us. And as we see through our spiritual eyes his completion of that awful ordeal, we will also feel the joy of the redemption of our own souls that he has brought about.

When I served as a bishop many years ago, people would often ask me, "When will I know the Lord has forgiven me?" I don't remember whether I had any truly satisfactory answers at that time other than, "You'll know through the Spirit." After my own experience with the Lord in Gethsemane, I now feel that we can most surely know we have been forgiven when we have been there with the Savior and pondered the meaning of his atonement for us personally. When each of us returns to be with the Savior in Gethsemane, we will know with certainty how much he loves us, and we will know with certainty, through the loving and peaceful confirmation of the Holy Spirit, that we have been forgiven.

These few verses from section 19 of the Doctrine and Covenants have helped me better understand why the Savior is so anxious for us to repent. He has dedicated his eternal life to our salvation, bringing about the means that allow us to repent, and he is anxious for us to forsake our sins, that the Atonement might be applied to those sins so we will not have to suffer the agonies he suffered. I think if we were not to repent, that would be the greatest of insults to our Savior. For us to be willing to accept and ask of Jesus Christ that he do this act for us and then to disregard it, to treat it as if it were of no worth or importance, literally means that the pain he suffered for you and for me was in vain. How could we put him through that?

The love he has for us is so complete that he will do everything in his power to help us cleanse our lives so we don't have to experience what he experienced. Like any compassionate children of God, if we know how painful something is, we'll do anything we can to prevent loved ones from having to experience it. All we have to do is act, to go through the process he has lovingly provided for us that we might be made whole. And as we have discussed in earlier chapters, having a broken heart and a contrite spirit is the essential, underlying foundation to the whole process, for, as Nephi taught, "unto none else" can his atonement fully apply and "the ends of the law be answered." (2 Nephi 2:7.)

And so we see the Savior standing at the citadel of the universe, having gone through an excruciating experience we will never be able to comprehend, but in a small way we can feel of his pain. We must accept him as our Lord and Savior, plead for forgiveness, and repent of our sins, and we can avail ourselves of this great atoning gift he has given us, avoiding the horrific experience that he, with great love, endured for us.

"GOD SHALL WIPE AWAY ALL TEARS"

It is good to look to the past to gain appreciation for the present and perspective for the future. It is good to look upon the virtues of those who have gone before, to gain strength for whatever lies ahead. . . . Oh, how much faith is needed in each of our lives—faith in ourselves, faith in our associates, and faith in the living God. . . .

If we as a people will build and sustain one another, the Lord will bless us with the strength to weather every storm and continue to move forward through every adversity.

—Gordon B. Hinckley

Despite all we do to understand, endure, and even avoid the pain that occurs here on earth, there are events and experiences in our journey toward our eternal home that simply can't be humanly understood. Out of the blue, we may be shocked by something that stuns us with its seeming randomness. It shatters our complacency and sense of security. And after the immediate stab of anguish comes the throbbing pain of an open wound that only gradually subsides and yet still lurks below our consciousness to surface at odd times as a pang in the heart and tears in our eyes.

May 18, 1995, was one of those life-altering events for

Gail and me. On that day, two of our daughters were driving back to our home in St. George from a shopping trip in Salt Lake City. Sharwan, who was twenty-four, had the year before returned from a mission in Argentina, and she was to be married a few weeks hence. Her older sister, Stacie, had accompanied her, along with Stacie's two-year-old daughter, Shilo. Gail and I had bidden good-bye to them in Salt Lake City just a few hours before. Sharwan was driving. As they approached Cedar City in Southern Utah, a terrible accident occurred. It was a clear, sunny afternoon with good visibility. Traffic was not heavy, and no one really knows what caused the car to swerve and roll. When the dust cleared, Sharwan and my granddaughter, Shilo, were dead. Stacie was seriously injured and was taken to the hospital in Cedar City.

When the accident occurred, I was driving to my office at Franklin Quest. My cell phone rang, and it was Gail, who was at the home we maintain in Salt Lake City for the times when I am there for work. In a choked voice Gail told me that Sharwan, Stacie, and Shilo had been in an accident. She had no idea what had happened or what the outcome of the accident was, but she said I should come home as fast as I could.

I remember making a swift and dangerous U-turn in the middle of a busy street and driving much faster than I should have to reach home. When I got there, Gail said that Stacie's husband, Larry, had actually been on the phone with Stacie when the accident occurred. As they were talking, he had heard Stacie shout something to Sharwan, and then the phone had gone dead. He was unable to reach her after that.

Fearing that there had been an accident, he immediately called the highway patrol and reported to them what he feared. Then he called Gail. At first we waited, but with no word from the police or Larry, we finally decided to call the Cedar City hospital. When I got the hospital on the phone, the person on the other end of the line realized she had to tell me that I had lost a daughter and a granddaughter and that my other daughter was in serious condition. She became extremely emotional and had a difficult time telling me what had occurred. The news of this tragedy was staggering. The pain of hearing that news was so great I felt as if I had been in the car with them.

We immediately went to the airport and flew to Cedar City. When we arrived, the rest of the family had already started to gather from various points around Southern Utah, and only then did we discover the full extent of the accident. Stacie was conscious but almost unrecognizable from the injuries and bandages. We stayed in the room for some time, not really believing what had happened but drawing strength from Stacie's living presence. When the hospital staff asked us to let our bruised and battered daughter rest, we decided to drive to our home in St. George, gather what we would need, and return the next morning.

Before leaving Cedar City, I went to the wrecking yard, just as the day was coming to an end, to retrieve what could be salvaged from the car. I felt as if I had been punched in the stomach when I first saw the devastating damage to the car. It was almost unrecognizable, and I marveled that Stacie had been able to survive. Even with all the pain and inner turmoil, I was grateful for that one bright ray of hope. As night descended on the countryside and in my heart, I was numb during my solitary, fifty-mile drive to St. George.

As you can imagine, this was one of the most painful, difficult times in our lives. Like most people, Gail and I had assumed our children would outlive both of us and that they would plan and attend our funerals. We never suspected that we would have to attend the funeral of any of our children, let alone our grandchildren. Even now, as I write this, the pain of the experience comes back like a stab in the heart, a memory I carry like a great lead weight.

In the harrowing days that followed, we decided that several members of the family, including myself, would participate in the funeral service. I struggled to prepare my remarks and had an experience not unlike the more recent one I described in the prologue about my struggle to prepare to speak at Elder Hansen's funeral.

The night before Sharwan and Shilo's funeral, I was sitting in my office in our St. George home. It was about two o'clock in the morning, and I was grief stricken. Just as in the later experience, there were so many unanswered questions— this time about why Sharwan, a young woman so pure, sweet, and wonderful, was taken just three weeks before she was to be married in the house of God. Why would the Lord allow her life to be cut short? She had so much to offer the world. And what possible eternal purpose could be fulfilled in this tragic loss? There were so many questions for which I could find no satisfying answers.

So, as in the experience preparing a funeral talk years later, I found myself wrestling with the purpose of life. What could I say at this funeral? How could I even speak coherently? My entire family would be there. Many lifelong friends would be there. What could I say to offer some solace and perhaps even strength to help us all—myself included—get through this ordeal?

As I sat in my office, my eyes wandered over the walls,

falling on a framed painting that has always meant a great deal to me. It is not an original piece of art but a print. It is not large, only about twelve by sixteen inches, but it portrays a poignant scene. As I looked at that print, I was drawn to it, and I got up from my desk, walked to where it hangs, and stood for a long time studying the scene it portrays.

The painting, one that has been reproduced in several Church publications, is a winter scene depicting a handcart company caught on the high plains of Wyoming by the early blizzards of 1856. A small group of travelers, pitifully clad in ragged clothing and wrapped in blankets whipped by the wind-blown snow, had pulled off the trail to bury one of their own, an all-too-frequent task that accompanied the wintry travail of those pioneer companies.

In the foreground is a family huddled around a shallow grave in which they had placed the body of an adult member of their family. Because the ground was frozen, the grave could not be deep, and in your mind's eye you can imagine the invisible, hungry gaze of the wolves just out of sight, impatiently watching the proceedings. The painting depicts the moment when the family is just about ready to cover the grave. The artist has powerfully captured the forlorn and windswept situation, the snow driven almost sideways, the gloom suggesting that night will be falling soon. There is no sign anywhere of a fire, of warmth or cheer, but only the relentless elements.

I had looked at that painting many times, mentally noting the sadness and remorse of this family having to bury a loved one there in an unmarked grave, on the plains, in a shallow trench in the frozen ground. But as I stood there that morning, before I would perform similar rites, burying two beloved members of my family, I saw something in that picture, something I had never noticed before. Far in the background, almost invisible in the falling snow, were the other handcarts and wagons, with the rest of the company giving the family their time and space to finish this sad task so they could rejoin the group and move on together, knowing there was safety in their fellowship.

I was deeply struck by the fact that in that little detail of the painting was the message. This was the message I needed to share and we needed to hear at the funeral. The pioneers knew something that all of us have to learn to survive the greatest challenges and difficulties of life: *Moving on is critical to survival.* In the painting, a loved one had passed away, and the rites of burial needed to be completed in spite of the blizzard and the cold. But the company also had to move on, and they knew that if they stopped for long, more people would die, and their situation would become even more precarious. Even with my own pain, I can't begin to imagine the anguish of that family as they covered that shallow grave, rejoined the company, and moved on into the deepening gloom. They had stopped, paid homage, and then, difficult as it must have been, continued with their journey as well as their lives.

And because they were willing to move on, they survived. Because they were willing to move on, Zion was established in the tops of the mountains, and the foundations of the kingdom of God were laid, enabling the gospel to be taken to the world. Because they were willing to move on, the Church has an amazing legacy that we look back on—in my case, of forebears who made my life possible because they were willing to move on.

As I stood in front of the congregation at the funeral of

my beloved daughter and granddaughter, I described the painting of the handcart pioneers and talked about moving on. Then I said something like, "You know, out in the parking lot are all of the wagons. These wagons are a little fancier than the ones our pioneer ancestors had; they move a little faster, and they're certainly more comfortable. But they are still wagons. And they are waiting for us to complete what we must do today and move on. When we get through this brief moment in acknowledging the passing of these two precious young women, we'll all get into our wagons, and we *will* move on. The Lord expects that of us. Survival demands that we move on. And if we move on in a way that is honorable and continue to live the gospel the best we can, we pay the greatest respect to those who have moved on in a journey different than ours on earth, and we can leave a legacy for future generations like the one those brave pioneers left for us."

That painting, and the insight it provided me, sustained me in that moment of suffering, and it has sustained me through much pain since. For the most bitter and painful of our mortal experiences, sometimes all we can do is simply move on.

So the message I would ask you to consider is really wrapped up in the title of this book: *Pain Is Inevitable, Misery Is Optional.* The fact is, we are not going to get through this mortal experience without pain. I have come to feel that one of the major reasons for being here is to learn how to deal with and learn from pain. How we choose to deal with it is perhaps the ultimate measure of who we are. And in my life's experiences, I am frequently reminded of my father's words before he died: *The sorrows will far outnumber the joys, but the joys will far outweigh the sorrows.*

We are not without power and resources to help us deal with the pain we experience. If we are willing to tap into that inner power that we came here with, if we are willing to internalize this empowering concept of a broken heart and a contrite spirit, if we're willing to listen to and heed the promptings of the Spirit, and if we are willing to move on instead of allowing ourselves to be stunted by the unfairness of it all, there will be no event, no circumstance, no tragedy, no sorrow that can drag us into despair.

Yes, there will be times, and there should be times, when we are going to hurt. But pain isn't going to ruin our lives; it's going to enhance them. Pain isn't going to color our attitudes; it's going to give us clearer Belief Windows and add depth to our personal portrait. Pain isn't going to make us quit; it's going to spur us on. Pain isn't going to allow us to make our own and others' lives miserable; it's going to encourage us to make our own and others' lives more bearable. Remember, while none of us welcomes experiences that bring us pain, we have the power to let it serve as an opportunity for growth and preparation for even greater battles in life.

It is my hope that this book has helped you understand some of these eternal and comforting truths I have come to appreciate so much. With you, I look forward to that day when our Lord and Savior returns to earth to dwell with his people and be their healer and their God.

I bear witness of the goodness and mercy of God, and I thank him for not giving up on me during my darkest hours and all the pain I felt. I testify that the atonement our Savior wrought for us is real, and that it provides the way for us to overcome the pitfalls and imperfections of mortality and take us home to our Father in Heaven. I thank both the Father and his Beloved Son for the painful but essential learning experiences I have gone through, and for the peace and blessings that have come once I reached out, took the Savior's hand, and let him lead me and tutor me and bring me back.

I also testify that pain, as difficult as it is when it comes to us, is a necessary part of mortality. But I also know the time will come when pain will be no more. It is my prayer that we may all be there and rejoice with our Savior when God "shall wipe away all tears from [our] eyes; and there shall be no more death, neither sorrow, nor crying, neither shall there be any more pain; for the former things are passed away. . . . Behold, I make all things new." (Revelation 21:4–5.)

INDEX